MEMORIES OF DONCASTER

TRUE NORTH BOOKS
DEAN CLOUGH
HALIFAX
WEST YORKSHIRE
HX3 5AX
TEL 01422 344344

THE PUBLISHERS WOULD LIKE TO THANK THE FOLLOWING COMPANIES FOR SUPPORTING THE PRODUCTION OF THIS BOOK

MAIN SPONSOR

CASE UNITED KINGDOM LIMITED

ALLIED MASSARELLAS

R&E ARNETT LIMITED

C BARNSDALE & SON

H&H BISHOP LIMITED

BRAIM & COOPER LIMITED

BROOK CROMPTON FRACTIONAL MOTORS

E&G CHARLESWORTH LIMITED

F CROSS & SONS LIMITED

DON VALLEY SPORTS

FOX'S MUSIC

PEGLER LIMITED

STRINGERS NURSERIES

RE TREM & COMPANY LIMITED

WALKERS SOLICITORS

WILFREDA LUXURY COACHES LIMITED

ACKNOWLEDGMENTS

The publishers would like to thank the following individuals and organisations for helping to make this book possible: Arjay Productions, DMBC Planning Department, Keith Deary, Doncaster Libraries, Shirley Eades, Empire View, Margaret Herbert, Steve Hill, JF Lawrence, Ralph Mann, The National Railway Museum, Sheffield Newspapers Limited, The Yorkshire Post, Valentine & Sons Limited, Donald A Wallis, Dawn White.

Introduction

Memories of Doncaster is a compilation of photographs spanning a period which focuses on the 1940s to the late 1960s. The reason for choosing this eventful time in our recent history is simple: *this* book is designed to rekindle memories of times and events which many readers of *today* are able to recollect. Consequently, this is not a book about crinolines or bowler hats - nor is it a local history book in the normal sense of the word. It has far more to do with entertainment than serious study.

I always expected that the compilation of this modest book would be a pleasurable experience, but in the event the satisfaction I derived from studying the lovely old photographs contained on the following pages went far beyond my expectations. Many different aspects of life in Doncaster have been covered in the book, as well as scenes featuring some of the town's best-known buildings. The subject matter ranges from local celebrations of national events - such as the Coronation and the V.E Day celebrations - to royal visits and exhibitions. A rare photograph of Sir Douglas Bader at the opening of the Excel Bowl in 1963 will bring back happy memories for many. Sir Douglas, the wartime fighter ace, lived in Sprotborough as a boy and was the inspiration for the film "Reach for the Sky." Street scenes are well-covered, views of the town centre which themselves are perhaps only memories are given prominence here. How many local folk will remember Clock Corner and the start of a first date with a loved one? Some of the pubs and cinemas which might have seen the next stages in many developing romances are also featured, and games of billiards and snooker above the *Burtons* tailors shop are also recalled.

Shopping scenes are included, and these are bound to rekindle memories of the sights, sounds and wide range of aromas which teased our senses as we toured the busy shopping areas. Like so many other towns and cities in the north, the heart of Doncaster has gone through tremendous changes in order to meet the needs of the national retail giants and the demands of the motoring public. The age of concrete and car parks was not universally welcomed, but the changes were inevitable as the case for relieving the town centre of volumes of traffic it was never

A trolley bus, silently moving along St. Sepulchre Gate, in the 1950s

equipped to cope with was compelling. Pictures of shopping scenes and shops which have long-since vanished are featured, along with the fashions and motor vehicles of the day which combine to refresh our memories of earlier times.

Many local companies have allowed us access to their archives in order to include their story in the following pages. These firms, well-known Doncaster names in their own right, are proud of their products and their people - and proud of their association with Doncaster. They provide us with a unique and often exclusive insight into the origin and progress made by these companies throughout their history. And fascinating reading it makes too. We are grateful to all the organisations concerned for becoming involved and adding to the interest and quality of the book.

The work involved in compiling *Memories of Doncaster* really has been a labour of love. Doncaster is a fascinating town with much to be proud of. It has been a pleasure to play a small part in recording some of the events and changes which have taken place here over the years and to bring them to the attention of younger generations who are becoming more interested and aware of the events and development of their town. I hope that you enjoy reading *Memories of Doncaster* as much as I enjoyed compiling it. Happy memories!

Kevin McIlroy
True North Books

First published in Great Britain by True North Books
Dean Clough
Halifax HX3 5AX
1997

ISBN 1 900 463 36 9

Contents

Right: *Nelson Street residents from the Hyde Park area of Doncaster celebrate V.E. Day with a street party in May 1945.*

Around the town centre

Above (small picture): It is hard to imagine looking at this 1920s view of Clock Corner that there could ever be traffic congestion, pedestrianisation, pelican crossings and the like. Manoeuvering your way across this junction seems to be no problem at all for cyclists, pedestrians and even the dog appears unperturbed by it all. The *No Waiting* sign at the top of St. Sepulchre Gate indicates there may have been an occasional parking problem but many years later this report appeared in the 'Doncaster Chronicle' in 1962:- *Steps are well advanced, it is understood, for a scheme which will drastically alter the centre of Doncaster. A block bounded by Frenchgate, Trafford Street, Factory Lane and St Sepulchre Gate will be re-developed privately in the near future.* The same publication states in August of the same year:- *Big scale development creates many problems and difficulties in the centre of Doncaster.*

Above: Clock Corner was a very popular meeting place especially if you had a date with a young lady or young man. Many a romance would get off to its faltering steps as a nervous beau waited for his lady to arrive by trolley bus or as it was better known the 'trackless'. Entertainment in the area was confined to the cinema and the pubs and there were plenty of the latter with the more notable ones being the Vaults on High Street, on French Gate the White Swan with reputedly the tallest bar in the country - it is said you had to be 6 feet 3 inches tall to be seen by the barman. If you wanted to take your date to the cinema you could choose the Picture House or the Regal or the Essoldo or if you fancied a stroll down High Street there was the Ritz.

Above: A pleasing photograph taken from the Trafford Street junction with French Gate providing a very interesting picture of this thoroughfare. The imposing building with the high roof and large columns is the Guidhall, the borough police station. It must have been a rainy day when this picture was taken for a policeman can be seen sheltering in the portico. To the left of the Guidhall was, and still is, a narrow arcade which then led to the registry of births and deaths and to the police cells, very handy if there was any trouble on Saturday nights in the Green Dragon or the White Hart public houses. The French fashion influence is evident with the hairdressers called Monsieur Marc, later giving way to Andre Bernard sometimes affectionately called the Mr. Teezy Weezy of Doncaster.

Below: Hallgate leading to High Street and on to French Gate was the leading thoroughfare in and out of the town. There has been little of the development experienced in other parts of the town centre and basically the only changes which have occurred have been to the use and ownership of shops and other buildings. The taller building on the right hand side was the Ritz Cinema. Entry to it was via an arcade which contained cafés and shops and this arcade could take 2,000 people queueing for the cinema which itself could seat 2,500 film fans. Opposite is the metal structure which was going to be the new Odeon Cinema but that never materialised because of the outbreak of World War II. The Ritz closed in April 1955 and re-opened as the Odeon in the following month before it closed in 1973 and re-located further up the street. The shell of the old cinema is still to be seen and the arcade contains shops but the hubbub of anticipation of eager cinema-goers has long since disappeared.

Below: Shoppers milling their way in Baxter Gate with this view going towards the market area. The ladies on the left hand side seem in their belted coats determined to be in fashion as they head up the street. Cable was then a retailer of very fashionable shoes and next door is Meadow's, the grocers. The public house at the top of the picture underneath the market roof is Beetham's, was named after its nineteenth century owners and used to have a six day licence. The recent changes to Baxter Gate have been concentrated on the left hand side with Binn's department store holding a very prominent position.

Right: The writer of this postcard complains bitterly to her friend in North Wales about four days of rain she endured at the beginning of her visit to friends in Doncaster. However, yesterday, Thursday, it was fine and she was able to get out to see the town. She would have noticed if she stood on this corner of High Street and Scot Lane on the right of the picture fine buildings leading up towards Clock Corner. The bank on the corner itself since the end of the last century was the Yorkshire Penny Bank. It had extended into Scot Lane in 1906 and up High Street in 1923. Further up is the National Westminster Bank built on the site of an Elephant Inn in the 1820s. Beyond that once stood the old Picture House and the last film was shown there in 1967 to be replaced by Bingo, so keeping with the trend of the times. On the other side our visitor would have marvelled at the Mansion House the home of the town's mayor and only one of three holders of that name in the country, the others being in London and York.

Above: Next door to the Danum Hotel stands Woodhouse Furniture Store. This building has lost a lot of its original nineteenth century grandeur when it was originally the New Bank. The original ground floor has disappeared and in the 1920s it underwent further reconstruction and blue mosaic tiles were added on either side of the first and second floor exterior windows and the premises became known by the name it has retained since the Westminster Buildings. Little explanation has been given for the change of name and even less for those tiles which are totally out of keeping with the style of architecture of the 1920s which can be found within yards of this place. It has been suggested that art deco took the imagination of the designers but it certainly does nothing for the building.

Probably the most interesting shop in this picture is the open fronted Mac Fisheries as the lady cyclist contemplates its wares. If you consider the competition from the many stalls in the town's fish market, shops like Mac Fisheries did well to survive. Its market style frontage is of note but also it was the shop which tried to tempt its customers with something different and became popular place to buy dressed crab and other 'exotic' items of seafood that we take for granted these days. Mac Fisheries also diversified into selling salad foods and it is said it introduced coleslaw to the people of Doncaster.

Right: The ironmongers, Wild & Sykes, is one of High Street's longest survivors and at the time of this 1950s photograph was still the town's main stockist of paraffin and gas mantles. It has changed little throughout the years and behind its rather inconspicuous frontage the selection of high quality specialist DIY goods makes it a popular place to shop rather than the supermarket like approach other retailers offer. The Lyceum cafe, next door but one to Wild & Sykes, is the same building referred to earlier as the original building of the Doncaster Literary, Scientific and Natural History Society. In fact it was better known as the Doncaster Lyceum. Here the building displays its Palladian frontage for the owners at that time in the 1840s wished to rival the Betting Rooms on the opposite side of the street for the grandness of its establishment.

Left: Looking down towards Clock Corner French Gate takes on a desolate air before the arrival of the ring road. This part of the old Great North Road passed over a culvert of the River Cheswold and this went underneath Jackson's Garage. As well as being the main Austin car dealers in the area, Jackson's gained prominence by being a check-point in the Monte Carlo R Rally at its High Street garage and for the Cheswold car built at the garage itself and named after the river that flowed underneath. This four seater touring car was a motoring connoisseurís dream and a real collector's item. It was a very limited edition and the very last one was acquired by a member of the Jackson family and displayed in the museum on Beechfield Road.

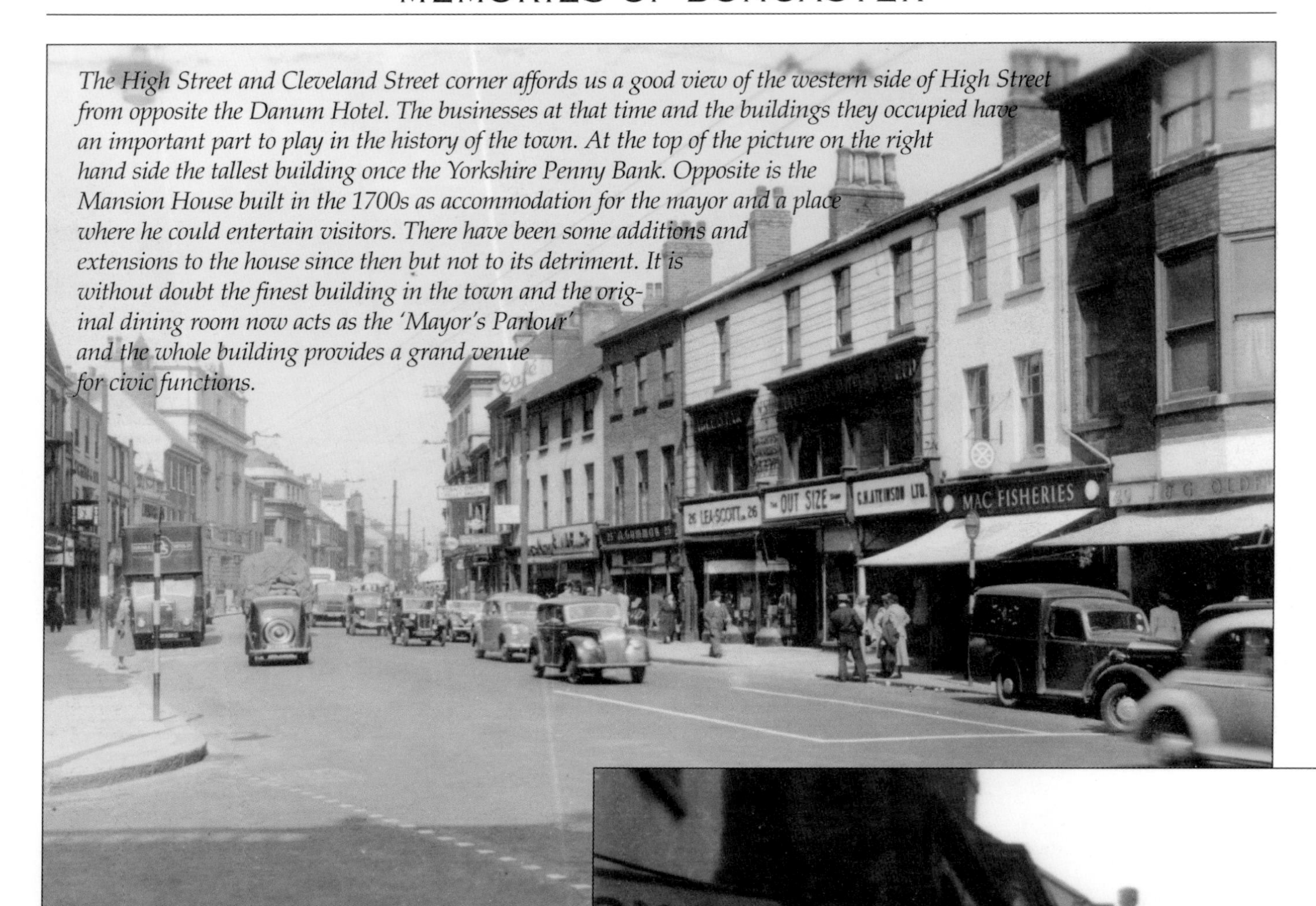

The High Street and Cleveland Street corner affords us a good view of the western side of High Street from opposite the Danum Hotel. The businesses at that time and the buildings they occupied have an important part to play in the history of the town. At the top of the picture on the right hand side the tallest building once the Yorkshire Penny Bank. Opposite is the Mansion House built in the 1700s as accommodation for the mayor and a place where he could entertain visitors. There have been some additions and extensions to the house since then but not to its detriment. It is without doubt the finest building in the town and the original dining room now acts as the 'Mayor's Parlour' and the whole building provides a grand venue for civic functions.

Above right: This is a general view looking with the corner of the Corn Exchange to be seen on the left. Out of sight behind the bus is the Black Bull public house, once owned by the boxing Woodcock family. Many of the original pubs in the market area still flourish and while still dependent on the market shoppers for their trade, are also busy at other times. The Red Lion, haunt of the splendid and eccentric Prince Monolulu, bears a plaque above the fireplace stating the origins of the classic race the St. Leger first run in 1776 although the total accuracy of the account is disputed.

This view of where High Street meets Hallgate at the Silver Street and Cleveland Street junction gives a brief glimpse of the building at the Silver Street corner opposite Pickerings of the Prudential Buildings. An old house dating back to the 14th or 15th century stood on this site until 1912. After it was cleared new premises were erected by the Prudential Insurance Company and their coat of arms is still plainly visible above the frontage although the building itself is now the home of a travel agents. Both the Prudential and the Pickerings buildings are fine examples of the 1920s style architecture with the rounded corners. Next to the Prudential is the White Bear public house which has stood on this site since 1779 with rebuilding having taken place over the years, the latest being in 1989. The view towards the top of High Street gives a splendid view of the Mansion House which seems to dominate the all the rest.

What is the lady at the bottom left of this photograph contemplating as she gazes across to the other side of Hallgate? Could it be that the Morris Minor car attracts her? Or maybe the two cyclists on drop handlebar bicycles being overtaken by the trolleybus reminds her that in Halfords a Raleigh drop handlebar bicycle will cost about £26. Unless she has been reminded that at home a doll needs repairing and the Dolls Hospital owned by the Meller family is not only just the place to have that done but also where new dolls and toys can be purchased. Is she wondering why the metal skeleton of the never built Odeon Cinema is still standing since 1939?

Left: The 'busyness' of High Street even in those days can be gauged by the need for traffic lights at the junction although it is safe enough for the cyclist to park his bicycle and safely cross still wearing his cycle clips. This part of High Street has been altered but not necessarily improved especially near the Silver Street junction and businesses such as John Collier cease to exist and have been replaced by frontages which do not enhance this part of Doncaster. The grandeur of the Mansion House just visible at the top of the picture remains one of the grandest sights in the town.

Right: This photograph gives a view of the junction of Cleveland Street with High Street and then across to Silver Street. The corner of the Danum Hotel is interesting as it moves with the times and advertises its Lager Bar. On the other corner stands Pickerings who sold radios and televisions and other electrical goods. At the bottom right opposite the Danum at the junction is the Reindeer public house, soon to be replaced by the Gas showrooms. The Essoldo Cinema on Silver Street in the right middle of the photograph started life as a theatre and retained much of the features of the theatre such as a lounge and even boxes down the side. The St.Leger Tavern closer to the High Street junction was a very popular meeting place at this time for racegoers, bookmakers and punters alike and is still a very popular town centre hostelry.

Bottom right: The redevelopment of Baxter Gate was a hotch-potch affair, with a mixture of modern buildings out of keeping with their traditional neighbours. As we look along Baxter Gate towards the market a new shoe shop at the corner of St. George Gate which led to the old library and the parish church of St. George is under construction and at the time the finished product appeared out of place with its surrounds, especially with the elegant frontage of Martin's Bank which can just be made out behind the van on the right. Soon to come is Littlewoods and Index but the traditional feel of the area is just maintained by the market and the Corn Exchange and the atmosphere they evoke.

Below: A fine selection of cars in this view of Silver Street as it winds its way towards the Market area from its junction with High Street. Memories will be stirred by the sight of a Morris Oxford, a M.G. Magnet, Ford Anglia and a Sunbeam Talbot as they are parked without hazard or restriction. The pedestrians crossing the road are in no danger of having to rush across to avoid the traffic and the photograph evokes a very sedate atmosphere. Prior to its widening in 1908 the street was no more then than a lane leading to Sunny Bar, Bowers Fold and the market and the view of the street we have here would be very different that then.

REINDEER VAULTS
IND COOPE
PETERS

The Wonderloaf
BAKED BY
GLENTONS of GRIMSBY
WJV 711

RATNERS
Jewellers of Repute
FARM STORES

RACECOURSE
BURTON

Picture: Sheffield Newspapers Ltd

Above: This photograph looking towards Clock Corner shows the contrast between what remained of the street and what was to be redeveloped later. The left hand side stayed very much the same with the changes which are not out of keeping with what was there before. The Elephant Hotel was a very popular meeting place for ladies and their gentlemen friends and is now the Yorkshire Bank. Further up the street William Deacon's bank has only changed its name, nothing else. It is now the Royal Bank of Scotland. Burtons, once grandly entitled *Montague Burton tailor of taste* retained its unique frontage with stone from Norway called affectionately but not accurately 'Burtonite'. A feature of many Burton's shops at that time was the utilisation of the spare space above the shop as a billiard and later snooker hall and Doncaster was no exception. The other side of the road fell steadily to the Arndale Centre and later to its enlargement into the French Gate Centre.

Top left: Clock Corner holds a very prominent position in the town at the junctions of High Street and French Gate and of St. Sepulchre Gate and Baxter Gate. The Midland Bank, built in Portland stone on the opposite corner has a copper clad dome with rainwater hoppers bearing the date of 1897. Across from there is the frontage of the Royal Buildings. That name at the top of this rounded building can still be seen. A real feature of buildings in the town centre where they stand at street corners is the round curved fronts and this junction where traditional buildings remain is an excellent example. Contrast that with the more modern developments on French Gate which appear to lack any style whatsoever.

Left: The trolley bus outside Hodgson and Hepworth is signed for the Racecourse. The sign for this bus and the one for Wheatley Hills, which left from the same spot, were in red in order it is said to indicate they passed the Royal Infirmary. This view from Duke Street towards Clock Corner shows the area which was to make way for the first phase of the redevelopment of this side of the street. There was a tradition of grocers, outfitters and shoe shops trading on this side of the road and names like Melias as well as Hodgson and Hepworth, Stead & Simpson and John Collier come readily to mind. The old style grocer has disappeared to the outskirts and been replaced by specialist shops or the supermarket yet the shoe and clothing shops continue to prosper.

Bottom right: This view of this historical part of the town is looking towards Clock Corner. The name, French Gate, can be traced to 1557 and before that in 1360 it was known as Frankysth-gate and in 1316 deeds show it to be Francis-street, deriving its name from a Franciscan Friary. The 1920s style architecture above the shops is much in evidence today in this part of Doncaster especially in St. Sepulchre Gate and High Street. What can be seen on this photograph has disappeared to make way for modern developments in the form of department stores and of course the Arndale, now French Gate Centre. The small shopkeepers and businessmen as reported in the Doncaster Chronicle in August 1962 were 'doomed', driven out by 'the big boys' because of high rents for the new premises.

Right: The first phase of the redevelopment of the area can be seen here with the old Parish Church of St. George hovering over the Arndale Centre. This view is from the Duke Street corner looking towards the new centre. The new Co-op, Danum House, at the bottom right of the photograph is the first building to be seen. The next building to be seen on this side bears on the clock tower the Latin inscription *Omnia Labor Vincit*, translated as *Work Conquers Everything*. At this time it was the home of the Public Benefit Boot Company, shortened as can be seen to Benefit. Cross over the road and the grandness of Hodgson and Hepworth stands out and following towards East Laith Gate these businesses, like Hather's butchers, all made way for the second phase of the Arndale Centre development. At the bottom left just visible behind the white van is King's Arcade with Jacob's corner giving way to the Red House of the Halifax Building Society.

Below: A comfortable crossing of French Gate for this lady and gentleman as they make their way towards the shops, maybe to Platt's for seeds or other horticultural or agricultural necessities or to the New Day furniture store or to Brough's for groceries. Only the White Hart is still there. These were the days before the compulsory wearing of crash helmets by motor-cyclists and this gentleman on his Trojan cycle, or popularly known as the 'putt putt', which to all intents and purposes was an ordinary bicycle with a small engine driving the rear wheel, is having a very comfortable ride towards Clock Corner and High Street.

Schweppes
HYDE
PARK

HAMMONDS
ALES
DONCASTER
BUTTERSCOTCH
SWEETS
&
CIGARETTES
CHEMIST
S.TRAVIS
DIRECT FASHION SUPPLY CO
CAFE

Below: As we look towards Hallgate and away from the town, we can compare the building in the centre of the photograph with the Prudential building directly opposite. These gas showrooms are an example of the changes which took place to towns like Doncaster at at this time. On that site until 1962 stood the Reindeer Hotel which was a much loved building and had been there since 1780 having been altered and extended in about 1837. Compare that also with the Danum Hotel which then still maintains its unique frontage. Up the hill from the gas showrooms still standing are the Dolls Hospital and it is interesting to note that further up once stood the second garage of E.W. Jackson & Son of Cheswold car fame and an official check point for the Monte Carlo Rally.

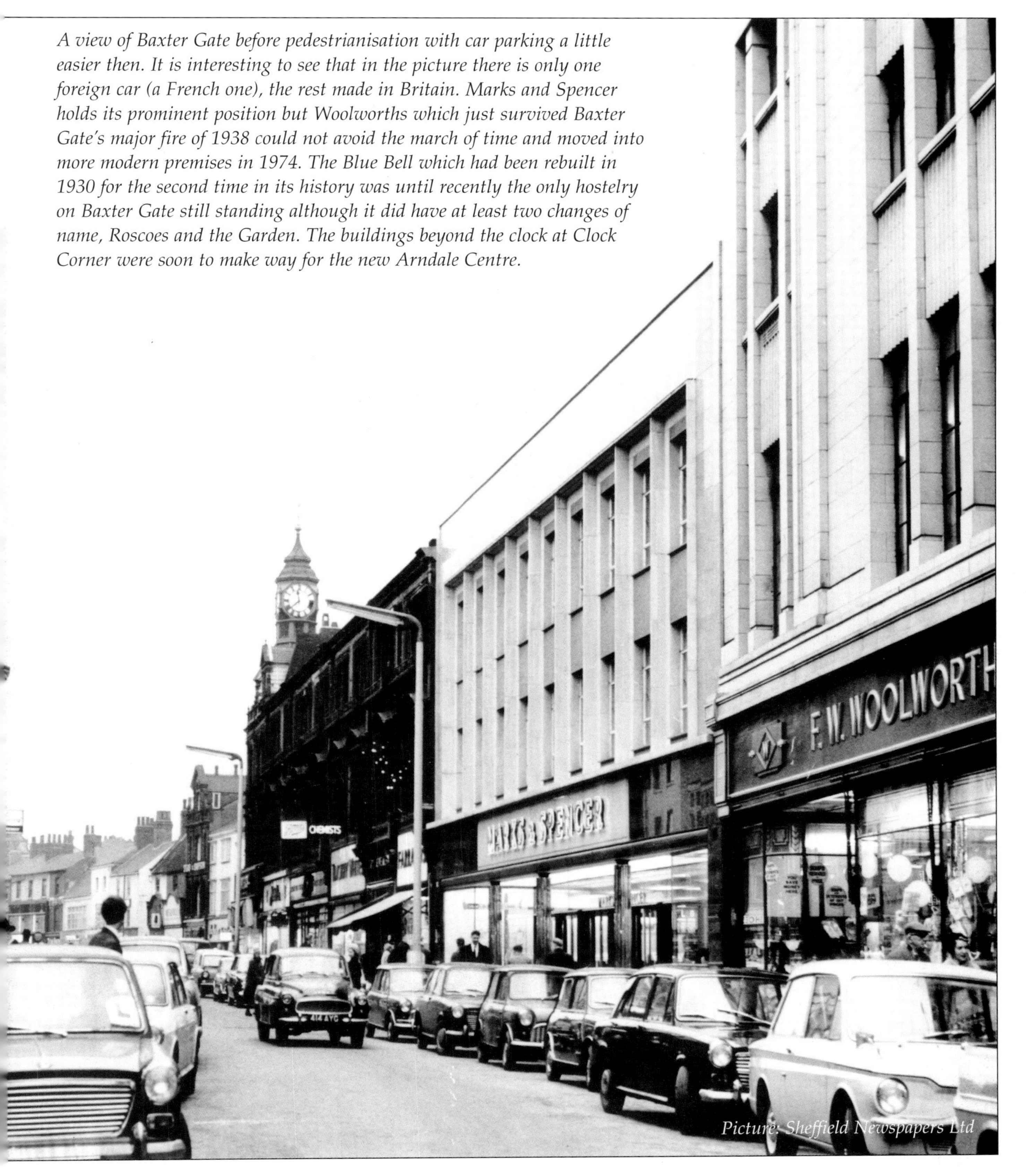

A view of Baxter Gate before pedestrianisation with car parking a little easier then. It is interesting to see that in the picture there is only one foreign car (a French one), the rest made in Britain. Marks and Spencer holds its prominent position but Woolworths which just survived Baxter Gate's major fire of 1938 could not avoid the march of time and moved into more modern premises in 1974. The Blue Bell which had been rebuilt in 1930 for the second time in its history was until recently the only hostelry on Baxter Gate still standing although it did have at least two changes of name, Roscoes and the Garden. The buildings beyond the clock at Clock Corner were soon to make way for the new Arndale Centre.

Picture: Sheffield Newspapers Ltd

Left: A view looking towards Clock Corner shows the beginning of the end at the Trafford Street junction and North Bridge to make way for the roundabout and ring road Soon to disappear will be the businesses on both sides of French Gate to make way for the shopping and business developments to come such as C&A, British Home Stores & Marks and Spencer and, of course, the Arndale Centre. The Guildhall is still here an imposing building dominating the street but that was soon to disappear. Jackson's furniture shop at the bottom left hand corner has gone and the junction will soon end at the White Hart public house. Looking at the volume of traffic in this photograph it would not take anyone much convincing that some kind of development would be needed to cope. What was of concern to many was what replaced the old and familiar.

GARAGE

Above: The bus station was opened in 1968 and this photograph gives a good indication of the changes that this part of Doncaster underwent in those days. There are some very interesting buildings still standing then. The centre top clearly shows Crimpsall Ings Power Station - there is the prison there now. To its front left is Gresley House but the railway station is hidden behind Sawyers Timber Merchants. Coming further down to the bottom left the imposing building is the Catholic Club. Below that at the bottom of the photograph stands the County Court House. At the top of the bus station site stands the colonnade of the non-conformist chapel and next to it the Pentecostal Church. At the bottom right on what is now College Road are the Swimming Baths and beyond that to the far right Christ Church Sunday School.

Left (both pictures): Situated on High Street on the old Great North Road this hotel was, and still is, situated in a very central part of the town. It was until 1909 the Ram Hotel and at this time was a very modern building with 50 bedrooms, bathrooms and a motor garage. On the opposite side of the road on the Silver Street junction is Pickering's who sold radios and later televisions. Even in those days High Street was a busy thoroughfare and the traffic pictured is heavy by the standards of the time. In the far distance is the 'Jewel in Doncaster's Crown', its Mansion House, the civic centre of the town. The external appearance of the Danum Hotel has not changed at all, the famous dome over the entrance remains and the buildings of High Street are not much different. Traffic lights are now sited at the junction but nothing much appears to have changed. The hotel has retained its popularity and is a good base for visiting football teams and is particularly busy during St. Leger Race week. Staff at the hotel look forward to race week for they receive good money tips if residents have had a good day at the races. During this time the hotel decided to move with the times and created the downstairs Planet Bar which was designed to cater for the 'younger generation'. The larger picture dates from the 1940s, the smaller, twenty years later.

Case United Kingdom Ltd - the company that moves the earth

Case United Kingdom Limited is much bigger than its plants in Doncaster. Its origins lie in other times and in other places. In 1842 Jerome Increase Case took a crude 'ground hog' threshing machine with him from Williamstown, New York, to Rochester, Wisconsin. USA. There he improved the thresher and founded the J.I. Case Company.

Soon he gained recognition as the first builder of a steam engine for agricultural use. During his tenure as president of the company, Case manufactured more threshing machines and steam engines than any other company in history

Case Corporation is a multi-national manufacturing organisation producing a full line of agricultural and construction equipment for the past 150 years. It has over 15 manufacturing sites around the world. Within the UK, Case has 1500 employees, 1000 based in Doncaster where their manufacturing operations produce 17,000 tractors a year as well as gear and shaft sets for 10,000 transmissions used in the Magnum tractor assembled at the Wisconsin facility in the USA

In 1985 Case, (itself owned by Tenneco Inc) acquired the agricultural assets of International Harvester who at that time had a long established relationship within the Doncaster area at the Wheatley Hall Road and Carr Hill manufacturing sites.

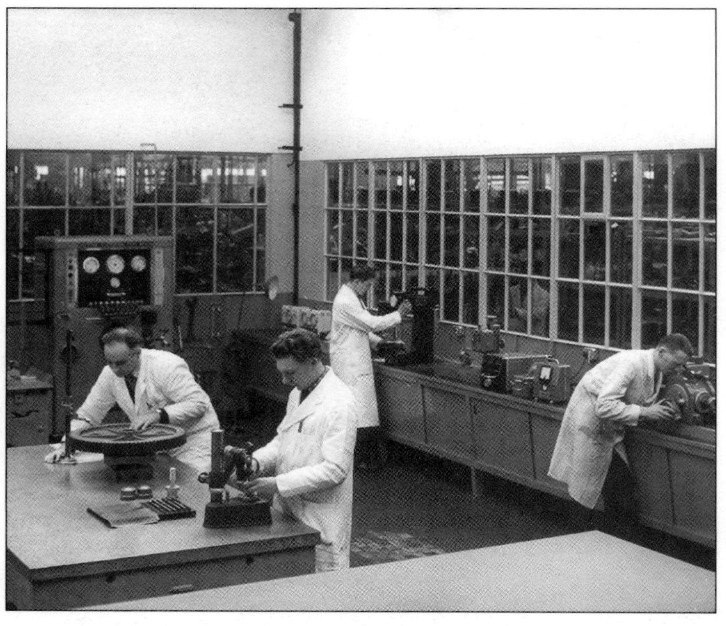

Above: *Work in the lab in 1959. Laboratory science was still in its infancy in comparison to today but the end results were just as good.*

Below: *The company's contribution to the Doncaster Engineering Exhibition in April 1948*

An early rival of Case was the International Harvester Company of Chicago (IH). It was in 1906 that International Harvester Great Britain was formed, just 55 years after Cyrus Hall McCormick, the company's founder, showed the world's first successful mechanical reaper at the Great Exhibition of 1851 at London's Hyde Park

The factory at Doncaster, which was built in 1938 was International Harvester's first factory in Britain. At the outbreak of war in the following year the government requisitioned the factory for munitions work and the production of jeeps.and it was not until 1946 that operations could begin. The earliest products from this plant were green-crop loaders,

At that time, IH in this country imported agricultural machinery from America and soon built up a successful business operation on this side of the Atlantic. IH imported some 3,000 Mogul and Titan tractors to the UK to help boost home food production for which the government personally thanked the company.

Above: *The assembly line in action in April 1956.*
Right: *The foundation stone laying ceremony on 7th August 1952.*

ploughs, toolbars and service parts for imported machines.

As accommodation increased, tractors were added to the range. The first British-built wheel tractor, a Farmall M, was driven from the assembly line in 1949 by a former Minister of Agriculture, who became Lord Barnborough.

In 1952, a diesel version of the Farmall M was made. Known as the BMD, it was followed two years later by the BWD6. Meanwhile, to meet the farmers' growing demands for greater mechanisation, pick-up balers, bale loaders, manure spreaders and harvester threshers had been added to the line and were in full production. The next year the first British-built International crawler tractor was introduced. It was designed both for agricultural and industrial applications and was to form the basis of the company's big construction equipment division.

Above: *The 'Christening' of the first all-British engine in February 1951.*
Below: *The proud workforce and the results of their hard work at the Wheatley site in April 1970.*

One of the Doncaster works' most successful farm tractors, the 55 horse power B450 was introduced in 1958. It evolved from the two models brought out in 1952 but because of its greater pulling power it won a good reputation in progress-conscious countries worldwide. It was also bought by British farmers who had heavy land to cultivate.

Another addition to the Doncaster range came in 1963. The B614 was the largest McCormick International wheel tractor produced in Britain. The same year saw a new 40 horse power crawler.

During the early part of 1965 all wheel farm tractor assembly was transferred from Doncaster Works to the newly-acquired Carr Hill Works, three miles away. Component parts for tractors were still made at the Doncaster Works but were sent by road to Carr Hill daily. This left room and freed facilities to cope with the increasing construction equipment business at Wheatley Road.

Above: *A Works' visit to the Sleaford branch of the National Farmers' Union in February 1950.*
Left: *Visitors try their luck at the 1952 sports day.*

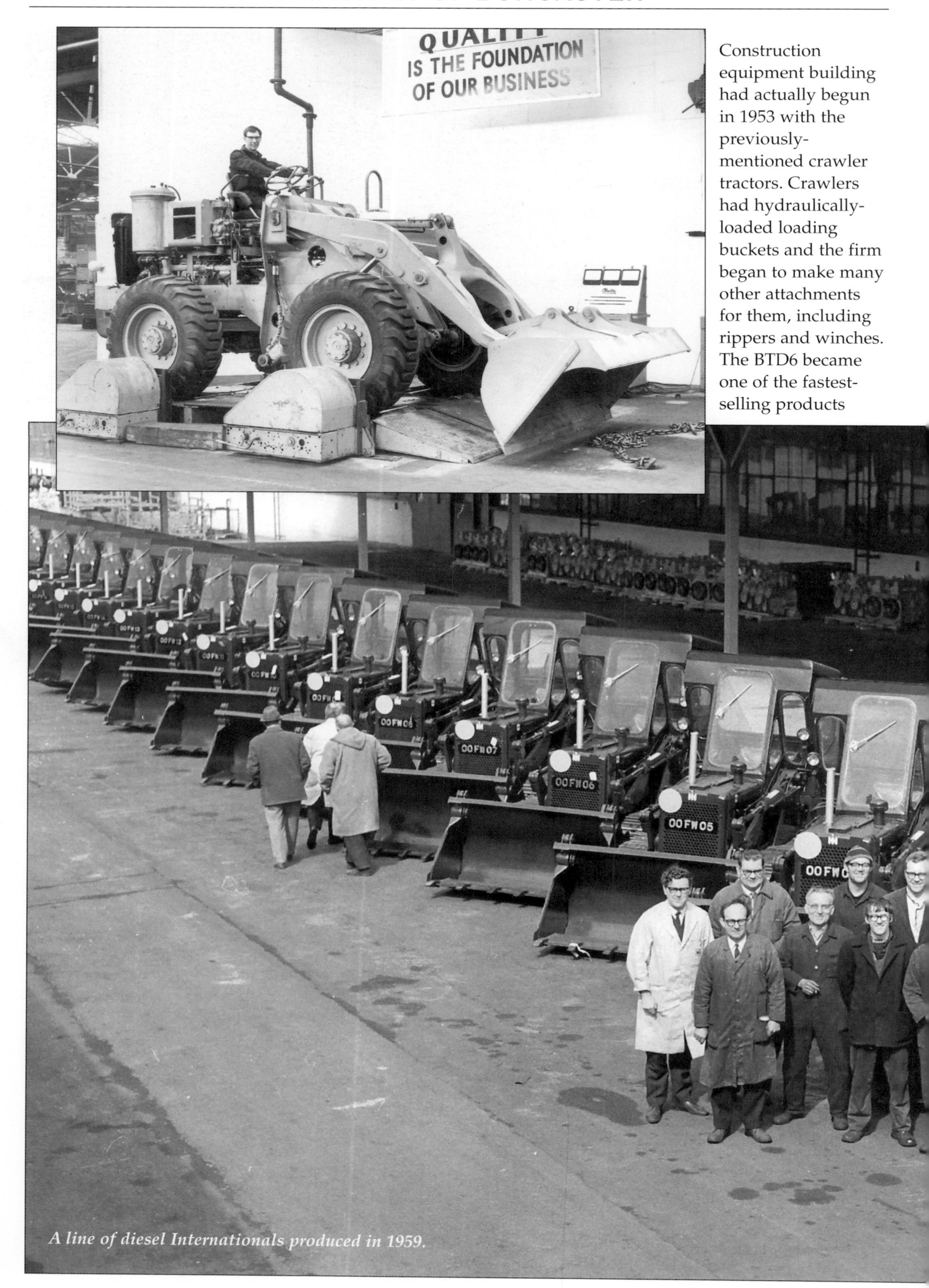

Construction equipment building had actually begun in 1953 with the previously-mentioned crawler tractors. Crawlers had hydraulically-loaded loading buckets and the firm began to make many other attachments for them, including rippers and winches. The BTD6 became one of the fastest-selling products

A line of diesel Internationals produced in 1959.

from the Doncaster factory. In all its versions it was exported to 60 countries in all five continents and also appeared on almost every major building site and road project in the UK. Its reputation was firmly established both for versatility and hard work. Its big brother, the BTD20 had 135 horse

Right: *An aerial view of the Doncaster Works in 1952*
Facing page, top: *A driver demonstrates a tractor at Wheatley in 1967.*

power and a 6-cylinder Rolls-Royce diesel engine and was in constant demand for all heavy earth-moving jobs. Progress continued, with equipment becoming not always bigger but better and more specialised.

In 1965 a new Parts Administration Office was opened to cope with the Doncaster Works' Parts Warehouse where orders were dealt with from a stock of 85,000 different items valued at £2,500,000

By the eighties the company was building a range of 16 tractors at Doncaster in the 50 to 89 horse power category. Its export record had been recognised on three occasions by the granting of the Queen's award to industry. Investment was running at over £25 million in the first five years of the decade.

The eighties slogan was 'Build Right First Time' and it represented a two phased programme. Phase 1 was introduced in 1982 and was specifically designed to produce quality components and assemblies that required no costly re-work.

A scheme known as "Pride of Performance" was developed to place responsibility for producing quality parts and assemblies directly on to each operator rather than leaving quality audit to inspectors on the line. The workforce rose to the challenge with an almost 100% reduction in rework. Defective work was channelled straight back to the operator or team responsible. Their job was to identify and rectify the problem themselves with the support of the technical staff. Special demonstrations were set up to show operators how the particular components they produced fitted into the framework of a sophisticated tractor assembly. A strong sense of co-operation and commitment was the result.

Truck production started on a regular basis in November and, at first, two vehicles a day were completed. Five months later a 540 feet long production line was turning out 30 a week. By 1970 this had increased to 200 a week or five trucks an hour.

Tractor assembly was scheduled to begin before motor truck production. During 1964 an 880 foot, elliptical assembly line was being prepared. Part of its length ran through a paint spray booth and drying ovens. Components for the tractors assembled came from Bradford as well as Wheatley Road.

Phase 2 involved the resiting of the assembly line in the major plant at Wheatley Hall Road, putting the two operations of manufacture and assembly together again, making a great saving on transport costs.

Carr Hill Works

The history of this site begins two years before wheel farm tractor assembly was transferred there in 1965. International Harvester Great Britain announced in October 1963 that it had acquired 300,000 square feet of premises at Carr Hill in Balby. A deal was struck that eventually gave the company 24 acres so that finalised plans for this plant provided ample room for motor truck production as well as the tractor assembly.

IH took possession and arranged for all necessary equipment to be installed so that a 1700 Loadstar, the first vehicle to be completed, left the factory in September 1965.

In 1982 the Carr Hill site closed, with the agricultural equipment assembly transferred back to Wheatley Hall Road, but only briefly. Four years later the plant was being re-opened by HRH the Duke of Kent, this time to produce the high precision/close tolerance ground gears and shafts for the Magnum tractor at 150 horse power and above. In 1992, Wheatley Hall Road and Carr Hill Plants merged as a one-plant, two-site operation.

In 1994 the company's major re-structuring programme threatened the Carr Hill site. It was proposed that it should go up for sale, be absorbed into a joint venture or, as a last resort, close. The workforce rallied round, set up improvement schemes and raised quality standards. There were two years of uncertainty before Leopold Plattner,

Above: *International Loadster trucks were built at the Carr Hill works in the mid 1960s.* ***Right:*** *During World War II, International Harvesters trucks were used by the Navy and Marine Corps. Here one is seen emerging from an LST.*

Case's European Managing Director, visited Doncaster, approved of what he saw and promised that Carr Hill would remain a part of Case.

Now, Carr Hill has been allocated nearly 20% of the company's transmission manufacture. Today, 12% of total sales comes through OEM business- developing specialised components for 'original equipment manufacturers.'

Case United Kingdom Limited

Because of Case's excess manufacturing capacity worldwide, a re-structuring plan was set up. Under it Wheatley Hall Road became a 'Centre of Excellence' for assembly operations. Its transmission assembly operations were transferred to an affiliate in France and the foundry closed in June 1997. A plan known as 'Future 11/Team Doncaster was implemented involving a large input from the workforce. Their ideas were used in the complete rebuilding of the assembly process costing 16 million dollars.

Case Corporation was launched when parent company, Tenneco decided to sell Case by floating company shares on the American stock exchange.

In May 1997, Case held an open day to mark the official opening of the new tractor assembly facility in Doncaster. The Vice-President of the European Manufacturing Operations for Case unveiled a plaque in recognition of the hard work and dedication of everyone who supported the creation of the new facility.

YOU are the HARVESTER COMPANY

This little booklet might well be entitled "An Essay on Friendship."

It deals with the advantages—or rather, the necessity—of friendship in business life.

In our private lives, none of us needs to be reminded of the value of friendship. Without friendship, we would find no joy in living. It is the number and quality of our friendships which determine whether our lives are drab or colorful, dull or interesting. That is why the normal man or woman is willing to undergo great sacrifices to make and keep friends.

The necessity of friendship in our business lives is equally real and equally great, although many of us are not so aware of it as we are in our private lives. Friendship or the lack of it may be the difference between happiness or unhappiness in our jobs, between business success or failure.

A business concern is merely an aggregation of individuals. The degree of friendship it enjoys with its customers and the public generally, depends on the capacity for friendship of the individuals who compose it. To the public, Harvester is you—and you—and you—for it is with all of you that the public deals every time it has a business contact with the Company.

Had you ever thought of it that way?

You and the Company, therefore, have a mutual interest in the good will of the public.

—1—

It seems that the Doncaster Assembly Plant has successfully accomplished the aims of its mission statement to be 'a customer driven manufacturer of agricultural equipment by meeting and exceeding the expectations and needs of all internal and external customers.

Above: *The cover picture of a booklet put out by the Public Relations Department of the International Harvester Company encouraging the workforce to present a friendly front.*
Left: *Throughout the history of manufacture on the site there has been a full social life for the workforce. Here are the Accounting Department winners of the Inter-Departmental Football Knockout Competition in 1950*
Top: *A very efficient production line from the 1970s.*

Events

The day for celebration; the day for the monarch's broadcast to the nation; the day for church services throughout the country ; the day for a holiday and for a party. And these children from Intake School and their teachers and maybe a mother or two are in the mood to celebrate Empire Day which was always April 24th. The flags of the Empire stand as proudly erect as do the children of the school in their fancy dress to celebrate the glory of the British Empire. The mood of the times was of patriotism, of respect for the

crown and for the achievements of the British people into gathering together within its protection lands across the world in all 5 continents for an Empire on which 'the sun never sets'. Soon after this 1950s picture was taken a change of mood takes quickly place ; the name *Empire* becomes *Commonwealth* as member countries become less dependent on the mother country and forge their own futures. The future, however, matters little to these children as they gather together to celebrate in their school playground.

Above: A very formal gathering this to celebrate the end of the war in Europe. The staff and their wives or husbands make a team photograph to mark the day. The lady behind the curtain seems to want to be with the rest but does not appear to be too upset about it. Everyone at this haulage firm looks happy enough and as they enter into the spirit of the occasion. The formality evident here will no doubt give way to the joy and happiness of the occasion and like the rest of Doncaster they can plan for the future. The only people recognised on this photograph are a Mrs Cliff, seventhth from the right on the front row and Margaret Shepherd, fourth from the left on the third row and beside her on her left is Joan Culver.

"ON VE DAY IN MAY 1945 THERE WAS A NATIONAL SIGH OF RELIEF AS COMMUNITIES WHO HAD SHARED THE TRIALS OF WAR CELBRATED THE END OF HARDSHIP."

Below: The residents of Nelson Street on the outskirts of the Hyde Park area of Doncaster proudly welcome their guests, the Mayor and the Mayoress, to their street party on May 5th 1945 to celebrate the victory of the allies over the Germans. This kind of celebration of communal rejoicing was very much repeated across the length and breadth of the land. There was a national sigh of relief as the communities like these, who had shared the trials of war together, should celebrate and share together. All it needed now was for the families to be reunited at last with the menfolk when they return from the fighting and to plan a future which only included the word peace. The feeling at that time was to ensure that the children did not have to endure what their parents and grandparents had to endure and the smiles on these people's faces gives that message of hope.

Smiling happy faces celebrate VE Day in customary style. After six years of war, peace in Europe is secured and the nightmare of bombings, air raids and husbands, fathers, brothers and uncles caught up in that bloody conflict is almost over. On this sunny May day in 1945 celebrations were nationwide and the residents of this Balby street were not going to left out. The flags and bunting came out of their mothballs, tables, probably borrowed from the nearby King Edward Road Junior School, were set out, chairs brought from each house and the children treated to potted meat sandwiches, jelly and custard, buns and lemonade. Afterwards games would be played, races, such as three-legged and egg and spoon run. The adults were determined that these children should have a good time and the spirit, so evident in communities like this, would ensure this happened.

Like almost every street in the country Haigh Avenue in Rossington was full of flags and bunting to celebrate the Coronation of the young Queen Elizabeth 2nd on June 3rd 1953. Once again the community spirit came to the fore as at the last coronation of her father and parties and special events were organised and here we see the eldest resident of Haigh Avenue, Mrs. Green, being crowned queen for the day. Despite it being June the weather did not behave itself and the day all over the country was quite showery. This Coronation was the first to be televised and gave the general public the opportunity to see the full procession and ceremonies first hand instead of relying on the radio describing the glorious occasion. For many people this was the first time they had seen television and it proved to be a forerunner of things to come as television brought the nation's great occasions to the people.

Picture: The Yorkshire Post

A very happy and youthful looking Queen Elizabeth II arrives in Doncaster to continue the tradition of royal visits to this September flat racing classic shortly after her coronation three months earlier. This tradition of royal visits to the race began with Edward VII when he was Prince of Wales in the late 1800s, continued when he was monarch and was maintained by his successors. Accompanied by Lord Scarborough, the county's Lord Lieutenant, and her racing manager, Lord Allendale, the Queen is smiling no doubt in anticipation of an afternoon's racing which she very much enjoys still, but also reinforced by the anticipation of her horse, Aureole, winning the big race. Unfortunately it could only manage third.

Picture: Sheffield Newspapers Ltd

This is a view from the Fire Station roof of the main racecourse car park. The raciness of Doncaster came alive during Leger week, more than at any other time during the town's racing year. The Market place, particularly every morning, was throbbing with life as shoppers mingled with tipsters like the befeathered Prince Monolulu whose pitch was outside the Red Lion public house. There were plenty other tips for the big race to be bought from ex-jockeys dressed to ride, all of whom would appear to have once ridden for His or Her Majesty and other jockeys similarly attired claiming that injuries had forced them out of the sport. The only way to savour the excitement and anticipation despite the number of cars in the photograph, was to walk to the course and to explain to your companions you had a sure-fire cert for the big race and tell them how you will spend your winnings. If you backed Meld ridden by W.H.Carr you would have been a happy punter on this day.

Picture: Sheffield Newspapers Ltd

Temporary crash barriers keep back the cheerful crowds waiting for the arrival of Princess Margaret for lunch at the Mansion House in 1964. It looks a chilly October day but the crowd seem patiently content to wait for a glimpse and a wave from Her Royal Highness. These were the days before royal walkabouts and over-exposure of the royal family and so such visits were occasions to be enjoyed and celebrated. The purpose of this visit was to open the new Museum and Art Gallery in Chequer Road as part of the redevelopment of the Waterdale and Glasgow Paddocks areas. This new amenity replaced the one at Beechfield House which had been demolished the previous year after serving the same purpose since 1909.

This is the London and North Eastern Railway stand at the Doncaster Engineering Society Exhibition held at the Technical College on 17th April 1948. Doncaster was a railway town on the main line linking London and the south with northern England and Scotland. The Great Northern Railway, synonymous with the name of Doncaster, became part of LNER in 1922 and from then the town was an integral part of the great age of steam. At the Plant, which afforded employment and training to thousands of employees over the years, famous locomotives

were built. There was the 'Sir Nigel Gresley' and the holder of the record made in 1938 for the fastest steam locomotive, 'Mallard'. Perhaps the locomotive which gave as much pride to the town then was the 'Doncaster Rovers', one of the many called after football teams. The last steam locomotive built in the town was a Standard Class 4-2-6-0 and that was in October 1957. It is a pity there is no railway museum in Doncaster for the nearest is in York and there are in the town small collections of priceless railway relics.

Picture: Sheffield Newspapers Ltd

Wartime fighter pilot hero, Sir Douglas Bader, bowls the ceremonial first ten pin bowl on June 5th 1963 at the Excel Bowl which was part of a large shopping precinct on East Laith Gate. Sir Douglas, who as a boy lived in Sprotborough where his stepfather was rector, lost both legs in a flying accident when he was at RAF Cranwell and was invalided out of the air force much to his great dismay. However on the outbreak of the Second World War in 1939 he rejoined the force to lead the 1st Canadian Fighter Squadron. His exploits as a pilot, despite his artificial legs, were the subject of a film Reach For The Sky and after the war he devoted his life to working on behalf of the physically handicapped and it was for this he received his knighthood.

It is May 12th 1937, the day of the coronation of King George VI, a prince not expected to be King until his elder brother, Edward VIII abdicated the throne rather than give up his relationship with the divorced American lady, Mrs. Simpson. In keeping with the spirit of the times it is time to publicly celebrate, to paint the kerbstones outside the house a patriotic red, white and blue, to display a sign saying 'Long Live The King' above the front door, to hang out the bunting and to have your hair bobbed in modern fashion, to dress up, to go to the street party and be happy. Looking at these two young ladies, fashions haven't changed much, have they?

Bird's eye view

The history of the Royal Infirmary at the junction of Thorne Road and Armthorpe Road is more in what happened prior to its opening rather than its building and subsequent developments. In the 1920s the land was council owned and at that time the miners of the area, because there was nowhere locally for any injuries to be treated in the event of a major incident, looked for a suitable place to build and decided on this one. In 1928 the site was opened by Lord Lonsdale, who owned many mines in the north of England, particularly in Cumberland. The same man opened the new building on 29th August 1930. During the Second World War those Italian prisoners of war, incarcerated on the racecourse, who needed medical treatment, would be sent to this new infirmary but were treated in wooden huts which each housed twenty-five beds. The exact date of this picture is unknown but it is thought to date from the late 1940s.

The spine of Doncaster dominates this 1958 aerial photograph as Hallgate and High Street runs towards North Bridge crossing the railway at the top. Starting from the southern end from South Parade with its many fine houses, cinemas seem to be the first topic. The Gaumont stands at the junction with Thorne Road and the Arcadia on the left at the top of Waterdale. The Odeon behind its arcade is the next to be seen on the right of Hallgate before the street meets its second junction with Silver Street on which can be seen the Essoldo, almost, it seems, backing on to the old Ritz now the Odeon. Coming back to Waterdale to the left of the Arcadia is the Girls' High School with the bus station further down. Behind the Gaumont is Christ Church. The Roman name for the town is recalled in the Danum Hotel where Silver Street and Cleveland Street meet and as High Street continues its march to the north, the Mansion House, the town's civic home, can be seen on the left with another cinema, the Picture House, on the opposite side just before Clock Corner. Here the street meets St. Sepulchre Gate and Baxter Gate and just off the latter on St. George Gate in front of the parish church of the same name is the public library. High Street has become French Gate before it meets North Bridge and the railway. At the top left on the far side of the lines is the Plant, the name for the railway works and the hub of the town's industrial life.

This is a fine view of the *old* Doncaster, centring on the Corn Exchange and the market area with the Wool Market on Market Road plainly visible to their left. Leading up from there at the very top left of the photograph is Christ Church and to its right on Hallgate is the old Gaumont Cinema. Below that is the Odeon Cinema with its Arcade leading to it. Across from there is Kingsway House built on the originally proposed site of the Odeon in 1957. As Hallgate moves towards the town centre into High Street past the Dolls' Hospital, the Reindeer Hotel and on the opposite corner the Danum Hotel, it is possible to visualise how important this part of the old Great North Road was in the life of the town at this time. At the top right the Cleveland Street and Duke Street areas come into focus with the Priory Place Chapel prominent and the co-op building just about to slide off the photograph before we move back to High Street to the top of St. Sepulchre Gate at Clock Corner. Coming left approaching the market is Baxter Gate and branching off left of that is St. George Gate with the parish church of St. George standing proudly as a vital part of the strength of the town. Like the previous picture, this view is from 1958.

Dating from August 1958 this is a very interesting view of Cleveland Street running up the centre to Silver Street and the Markets. Parallel to it is Waterdale with the old bus station in the bottom right-hand corner. At the top of the station is Priestnall's café and on the opposite side stands Honor Bright's newsagents. Wood Street links Waterdale with Cleveland Street and just up from that is Hallgate joining Cleveland Street at the Reindeer Vaults. Coming back down past Printing Office Street we meet Duke Street with a very fine view of the new Co-op, Danum House, as it reaches St. Sepulchre Gate at the bottom of which is Newton's Fish and Chip shop. To the rear of the Co-op is Priory Place Chapel and leading back to High Street on Priory Place itself is the Post Office built in 1885. At the very top are the Gas Works and, coming past the Pig and Cattle Markets, is the Flour Mill on the banks of the Don with the parish church in front.

Seven sets of railway lines converge on Doncaster and here we can see how it earned the name of 'Railway Town'. Gresley House had just been built at this time replacing some cottages. Two very interesting buildings here are the Grand Theatre and the West Riding Police Station. Station Road, which acted as one the main links between the town centre and the railway station directly opposite, housed the white fronted theatre which later survived plans to demolish it after public protest. The bleak looking police headquarters face the Railway Station but when the borough and county police merged a new police station was built on the Waterdale site. Factory Lane is still a prominent thoroughfare at this time from Trafford Street to St. Sepulchre Gate at its junction with West Laith Gate where the Quaker Meeting House and the famous Bee Hive pub stood. The bottom of the photograph shows the roof of Danum House on Duke Street and opposite are Jacob's corner and King's Arcade with Hodgson and Hepworth on St. Sepulchre Gate before that popular store was swallowed up in the clearances for the new shopping centre, the beginnings of which can be seen in the middle right. The picture dates from October 1963.

This photograph shows the initial stages of the redevelopment of the western side of Doncaster with the new inner ring road, Trafford Way, turning Trafford Street into a dual carriageway between its junction with Cleveland Street and French Gate. This entailed the relocation of businesses like Sawyers Timber Merchants to the new road just below the railway station. The railway lines, which seem to centre on the town, and the railway works dominate the left hand side, with the roof of Gresley House almost overshadowing the railway station. Towards the top of the photograph in the River Don New Cut basin is the Rank Flour Mill with the parish church of St. George standing out in front, looking across to the market and the Corn Exchange. St. Sepulchre Gate winds its way up the centre, pausing at the new Trafford Way. The fine new Co-op at the Duke Street junction is the first of the street's many imposing buildings in view. Almost opposite is Harry Jacob's corner, with Hodgson and Hepworth on the same side, then the new Arndale Centre before it meets High Street and French Gate at Clock Corner. The date of this picture is unknown.

Trafford Way has now been extended at the North Bridge end into Church Way, almost, it appears, cutting off St. George's church from the rest of the town. The new road has by this time extended to Wheatley turning the once busy Dockin Hill Road on the top right of the last round-about into a quiet lay-by. There is a good view of the Rank flour mill on the Don and coming across Greyfriars at the junction with Church Way is the old Technical High School before it was moved to Intake although the building did itself become part of the Doncaster College. Another fine sight is the roof of the Corn Exchange, scene of so many exciting moments in the life of the town, with the adjoining covered market and the whole of the market area including the cattle and pig markets close by. As with the previous picture, the date of this photograph is unknown.

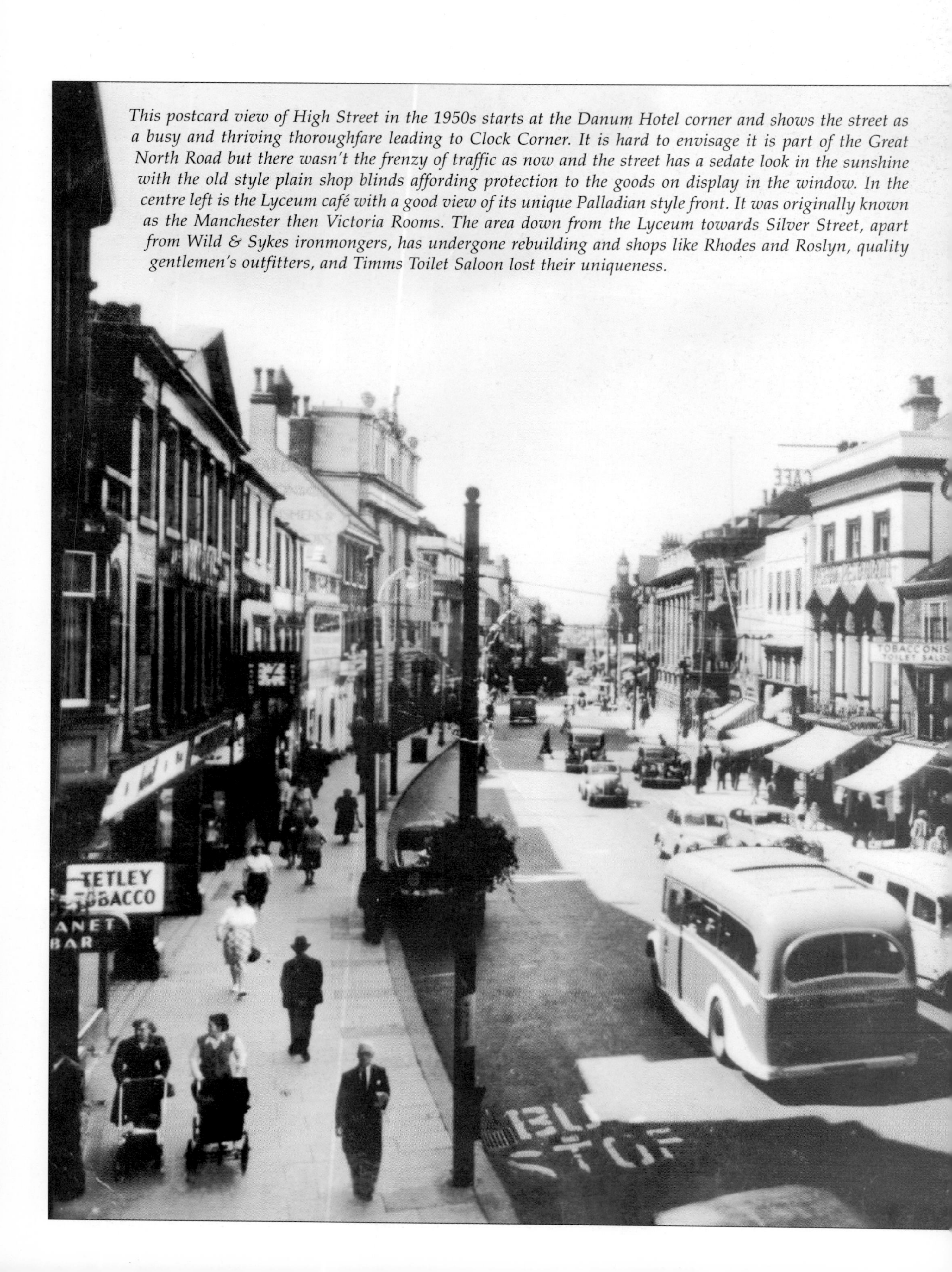

This postcard view of High Street in the 1950s starts at the Danum Hotel corner and shows the street as a busy and thriving thoroughfare leading to Clock Corner. It is hard to envisage it is part of the Great North Road but there wasn't the frenzy of traffic as now and the street has a sedate look in the sunshine with the old style plain shop blinds affording protection to the goods on display in the window. In the centre left is the Lyceum café with a good view of its unique Palladian style front. It was originally known as the Manchester then Victoria Rooms. The area down from the Lyceum towards Silver Street, apart from Wild & Sykes ironmongers, has undergone rebuilding and shops like Rhodes and Roslyn, quality gentlemen's outfitters, and Timms Toilet Saloon lost their uniqueness.

Shopping Spree

A wet night in the 1950s looking down St. Sepulchre Gate towards Duke Street on the left of Harry Jacobs furniture store with the illuminated sign on top of the building urging the use of electricity. This corner was another favourite meeting place for courting couples and they could then progress later to the registrar of marriages on the first floor of the King's Arcade which was to the rear of Harry Jacobs. An office of the Halifax Building Society was built on that site when it was demolished. Outside Hodgson and Hepworth was a trolley bus waiting area to Wheatley Hills and the Racecourse. The bus itself in the picture is advertising the famous Doncaster made treat of Nuttall's Mintoes which vied with Doncaster Butterscotch as the local children's and adult's special weekend treat.

HODGSON & HEPWORTH
NUTTALL'S
MINTOES

Above: Hodgson & Hepworth Ltd, the Fortnum's of Doncaster opened in 1877 in St. Sepulchre Gate and remained there as a familiar landmark until it was demolished to make way for the new shopping centre. This was a quality store and prided itself on the personal counter service it provided for its customers and the range and quality of its products. It was a place to see and be seen with the café with its tiny stage for a three-piece orchestra overlooking the busy street a popular venue to meet friends. Customers were not allowed credit - it was a ready money store. On entering the shop the smells of smoked ham and of freshly ground coffee was described by one admirer as 'succulent'. That may not be the technically correct word but probably the most descriptive and memory evoking.

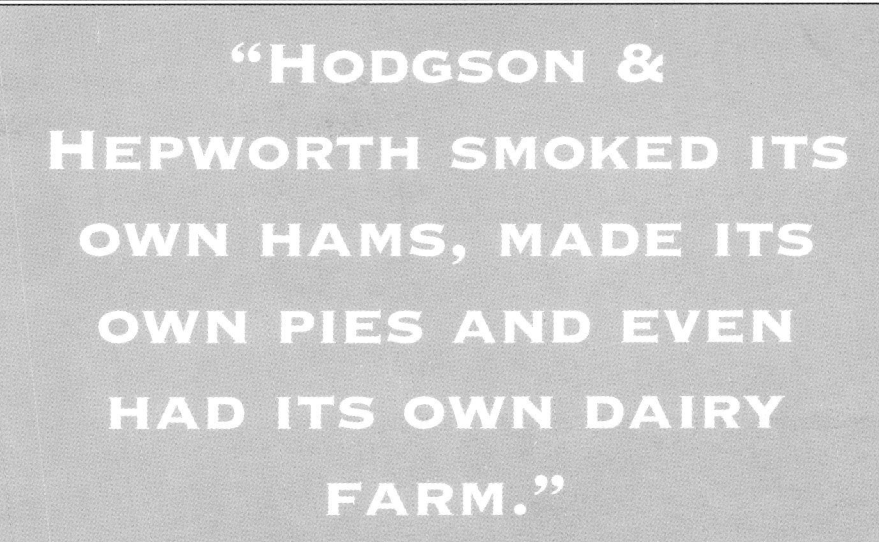

"HODGSON & HEPWORTH SMOKED ITS OWN HAMS, MADE ITS OWN PIES AND EVEN HAD ITS OWN DAIRY FARM."

Below: The enticing aroma of the shop is brought out by this picture of hams, bacons, flitches, pork pies and all the foods synonymous with the name of Hodgson & Hepworth. Coffee from all over the world was ground on the premises, the shop smoked its own hams, made its own pies and even had its own dairy farm. The counter service for which it was renowned is a central part of this photograph. The metal railing which stretched the length of the counter was unique. Who can remember the weighing scales with the ounces and pound weights glistening next to the scales as they measured out sugar and the poured it into the traditional blue sugar bag? Or the flour, weighed and wrapped up securely in a white cotton bag? Or the fresh yeast on a slab, cut off and weighed and wrapped in paper ready for a spot of home baking?

Above: The Doncaster Mutual Co-operative Industrial Society Limited was better known as the Co-op or the Store. Headquarters here is on the corner of St. Sepulchre Gate and Duke Street. In 1950 there were 44 Co-ops within the range of fifteen miles of the town centre and that was later increased to 68. If you wanted it, the Co-op would have it! The Co-op offered a personal service. Each member, and nearly everybody was one, had their own Co-op number. That number was recited each time a purchase was made ready for when the Society paid out its dividend to members on 'divvy' day. All Doncaster Co-op buildings have been impressive, leading the way in distinctive and attractive architecture and it is a relief to know that this building still remains a part of Doncaster although for a slightly different use.

"In 1950 there were 44 Co-ops within a range of fifteen miles of the town centre."

Below: The new Co-op opened in 1938 in St. Sepulchre Gate opposite the old building. It is said that Lord Haw Haw (William Joyce) threatened in one of his broadcasts that the German Luftwaffe would bomb the Co-op. It never did but there was a near miss. This modern Co-op was originally called The Emporium but after a public competition in the 1970s Danum House was chosen. There was a ballroom on the third floor and many popular bands played there, including Eric Delaney's and Johnny Dankworth's with Cleo Laine as vocalist. The resident orchestra was led by Frank Cornish with the maestro himself noted for a very romantic last waltz played on his violin.

Below: The parish church of St. George is the backdrop to this 1940s photograph of the market area looking north with Baxter Gate in the top left hand corner. The covered market and Corn Exchange are at the right-hand side and the view of the stalls towards Baxter Gate ends at the Fish Market which was refurbished in 1973. Most of the buildings in front of the church were soon to disappear in the redevelopment of the area. This bottom part of the market attracted great crowds during race weeks, particularly in September for the St. Leger. One favourite was Prince Monolulu, dressed in his ostrich feathers, shouting *"I've gotta horse!"* from outside the Red Lion public house. Another entertainer there at the same time was an escapologist who always managed to miraculously escape from his chains at the very last death-defying moment.

"THE BOTTOM PART OF THE MARKET ATTRACTED GREAT CROWDS DURING RACE WEEKS, PARTICULARLY FOR THE ST. LEGER."

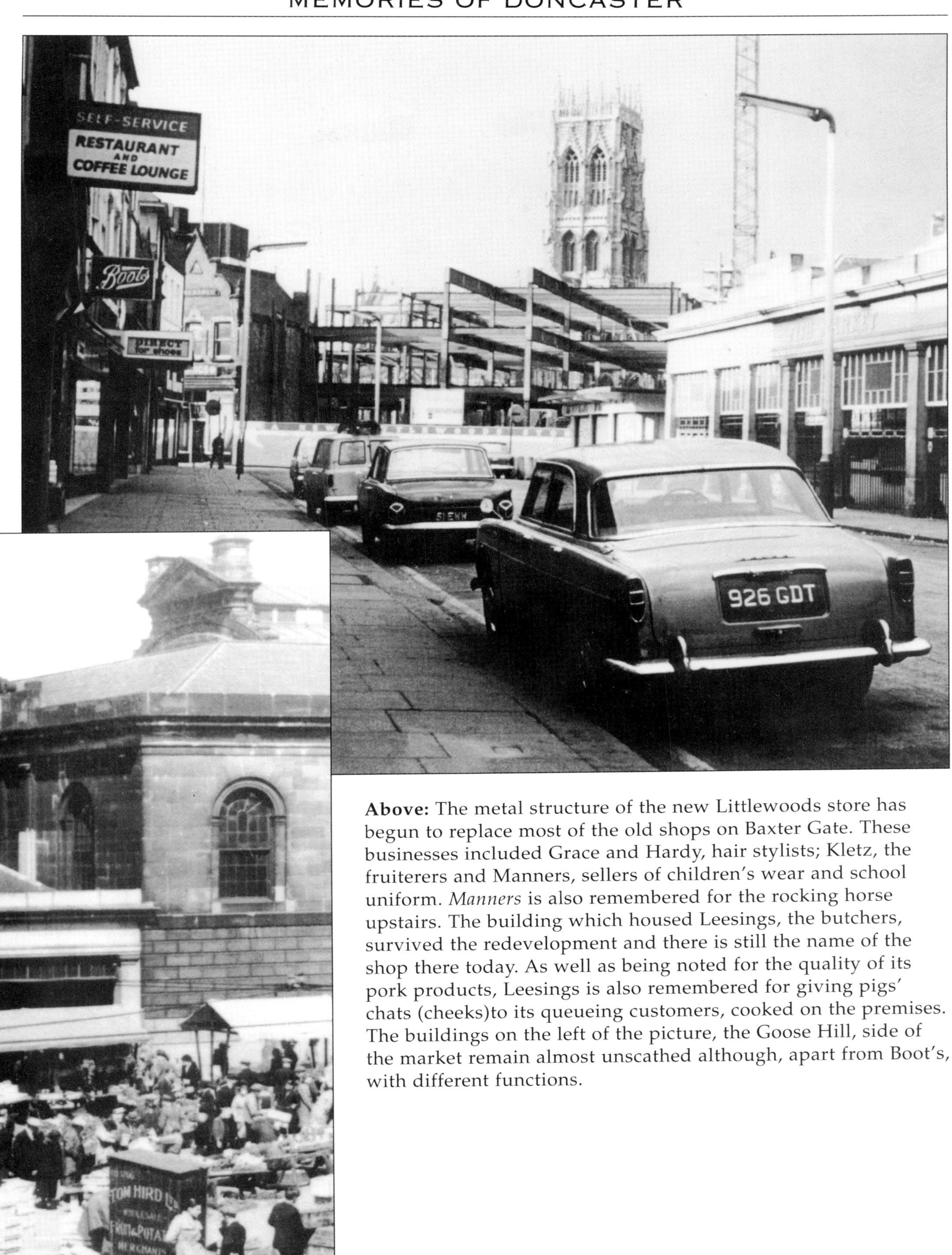

Above: The metal structure of the new Littlewoods store has begun to replace most of the old shops on Baxter Gate. These businesses included Grace and Hardy, hair stylists; Kletz, the fruiterers and Manners, sellers of children's wear and school uniform. *Manners* is also remembered for the rocking horse upstairs. The building which housed Leesings, the butchers, survived the redevelopment and there is still the name of the shop there today. As well as being noted for the quality of its pork products, Leesings is also remembered for giving pigs' chats (cheeks)to its queueing customers, cooked on the premises. The buildings on the left of the picture, the Goose Hill, side of the market remain almost unscathed although, apart from Boot's, with different functions.

Above: Children here are enjoying a welcome diversion on the roundabout situated at the north side of the very busy market. This attraction regularly attended the market and competed for attention with the many stalls selling anything and everything. The noise of the stallholders advertising their wares was especially noticeable and at this part there was an especially enthusiastic vendor of carpets whose voice seemed to outshout the rest. Tuesday, Friday and Saturday were market days with Tuesday given also to livestock day when pigs were either sold on or sent to the nearby abattoir where their protesting squeals seemed to pierce the noise and hullabaloo of the rest of the market activities.

Above right : These ladies who don't seem to think that 5/11 is a fair price to pay for these works of art. The dresses, hats, cardigans of the ladies and the suits, collar and ties of the men contrast strongly the casual wear of shoppers today. The sturdy public toilets in the background look modern, although the conservation order could not have meant them.

Right: The crowd of people and children gathered near the roundabout was typical of the numbers who attended one of the biggest, if not *the* biggest in Yorkshire. Halls were set aside for the selling of fish, vegetables, fruit and other local produce. As today the stalls opened on to he street with the central hall on the inside and the famous Corn Exchange next door. The area has remained virtually unchanged with plans after World War II to develop the area thus demolishing many fine buildings never being carried out. The market area was declared a conservation area in 1973 much to the relief of those who felt the old market and its traditions were worth saving.

Below: The first sighting of the 'changing face of Doncaster' as the local newspapers at the time used to report. This is the new Arndale Centre which stood at the corner of French Gate and St. Sepulchre Gate and was opened in 1964. The centre contained the notorious (some say) statue entitled Ecstasy which depicted a naked male and female together. It did cause a great deal of controversy with a great many views held and volubly expressed from total abhorrence to admiration as a 'work of art' to 'I don't know what the fuss is about'. However the 'antis' seem to have had their way and Ecstasy was eventually replaced by something less controversial as the centre was extended and re-named the French Gate Centre.

Picture: Sheffield Newspapers Ltd

Above: St. Sepulchre Gate has had various names since 1372, all closely connected with its present title but it appears nothing to do with any saint at all. The street developed into a major centre of trade and business and as Doncaster grew so did St. Sepulchre Gate in economic stature. The shops which traded on this site prior to the extension or the Arndale Centre into the French Gate Centre examples of the diversity of trade to be found in the town. Bell Bros. the jewellers is a good example of a shop which could stand the march of time since it began trading in the street in about 1853. Other shops in the vicinity included Stead and Simpson, boot and shoemakers; the Stylo Boot Company; John Collier, tailor with 'the window to watch', Lucille Gowns, Dewhirst the butchers and the tailors, Weaver To Wearer. There were others like Hodgson and Hepworth, True-Form and Melias all swallowed up in the name of progress.

Smart
Weston

This is a view of the Market area looking south-east from Baxter Gate towards the Corn Exchange with the stalls of the Fish Market at the corner behind Masserella's ice cream stall. To the right of the fish market are the general stalls. Hilton's shoe shop is on the corner of the old Goose Hill and Baxter Gate. The 'jewel in the crown' is undoubtedly the Corn Exchange built in 1873 and the centre for political rallies, boxing and wrestling, musical concerts involving bands, orchestras and choirs, particularly those involving local school children. Bruce Woodcock would have boxed here at the start of his career in the 1940s and the famous Welsh politician, Nye Bevan, displayed his oratorical skills to a full house of 1600. The hall was badly damaged by fire in 1994 and was re-opened in August 1997 back to its former glory with shops and arcades though with less seating capacity.

Don Valley Sports - from modest ambitions.....

Whilst working as a young man for the Kilnhurst Co-op as a shoe-repairer, Marshall Cutts already had ambitions to own his own business and began by mending neighbours' shoes in a small shed at the bottom of his garden.

By adding his limited savings to the proceeds of the sale of his precious BSA motor bike, he managed to raise the £250 he needed to put down a deposit on his first business. He bought it from a Mr Ernest Weston of Bank Street, Mexborough. The balance had to be paid over the following eighteen months. Since his first week's takings were just £10, Marshall realised that a great deal of hard work would be required if he were to meet the repayments.

The shop's small window displayed the leather and fancy goods for sale. In the late summer of 1953, Marshall experimented with the sale of imported tennis racquets. Thus began the gradual

shift from repairing shoes to selling sports equipment.

In the same year, Marshall married and after a further two years his wife joined him in the business. It did so well that by 1955 the tiny shop at 80B Bank Street could not contain all the stock and a second shop was opened in Bank Street on

Above: *Camping and outdoor Pursuits Centre at Littleworth Lane, Old Rossington.* ***Left and below:*** *Emlyn Hughes signs copies of his book 'Fit Hit' at the opening of the High Street branch in 1979.*

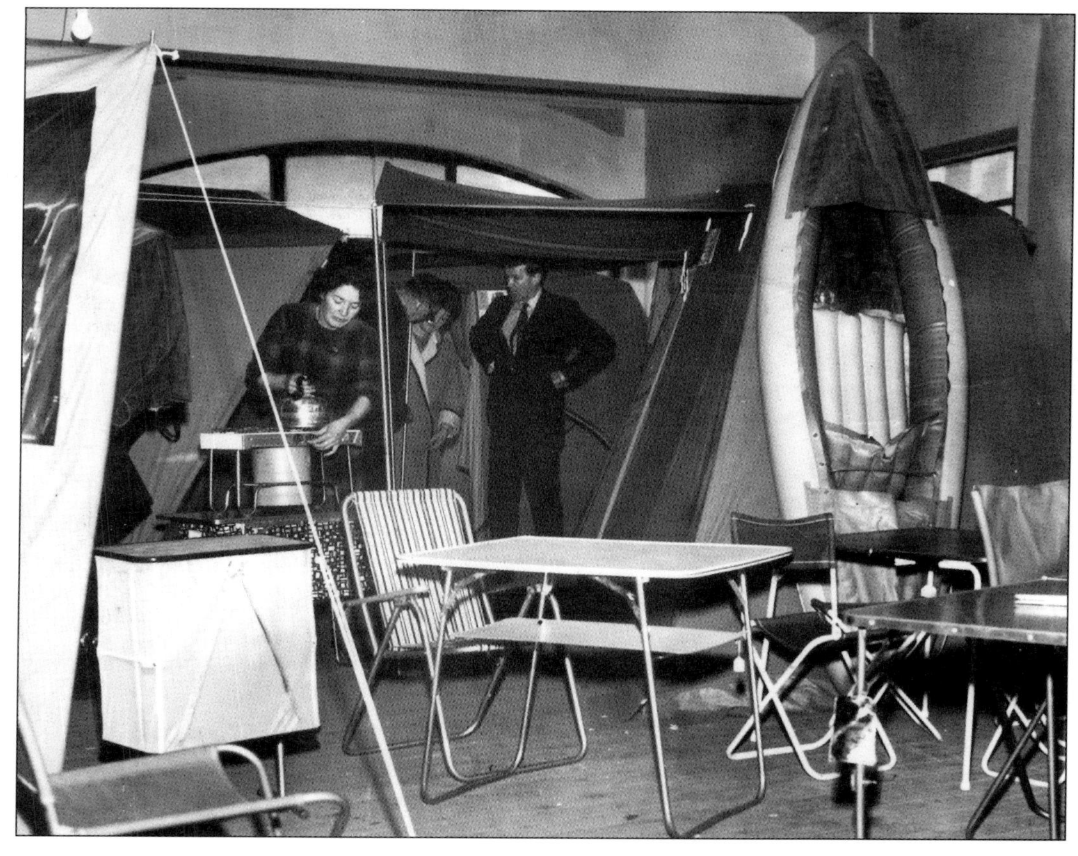

the site of the present flyover.

A demand for camping gear encouraged Marshall to add this to his range and, by 1958, the company was putting on camping exhibitions in various venues. Pictured is one of the earliest at the Free Christian Hall, Mexborough in 1959.

This side of the business grew rapidly until, in 1967, a separate Outdoor Pursuits Centre was established on land purchased in 1967 at Littleworth Lane, Old Rossington. Here there is a permanent exhibition of tents, outdoor clothing and ski and swim wear. Ski training takes place each winter and a full repair service is offered for tents and awnings and skiing equipment.

The sports side of the business continued to expand with shops opening in Barnsley in February 1960 and at St Sepulchre Gate, Doncaster in the same year. The present shop in High Street, Mexborough was opened in 1976, having moved from Bank Street.

In 1962 Mr and Mrs Webb, relatives of Mr and Mrs Cutts, staying with them through the formative years, managing the Mexborough shop until their retirement in 1995.

The Cutts' daughter, Heather, joined the company in 1974, eventually becoming a partner.

1979 saw the opening of 10, High Street, Doncaster under the new name, Fitkit. The present St Sepulchre Gate premises were bought from Cantors after a disastrous fire in 1986 and refurbished. The company opened there in 1989, moving from Spring Gardens.

Mr Cutts has now relinquished his interest in the sports shops to concentrate on, and expand the Outdoor Centre at Old Rossington.

Above: *A picture taken at the Free Christian Hall in 1959. Heather, the Cutts' daughter is in a carry-cot in one of the tents.*
Left: *The shop in Spring Gardens which the business occupied between the years 1965 and 1989.*

Music for every generation

Charles J Fox, the firm's founder, born in 1866, was a Lancashire man. As a young man he bought a cheap piano, which was all he could afford, restored it and sold it to an admiring neighbour. Realising he could make a living this way, he opened a shop in Burnley, then took larger premises in Leeds where he sold all sorts of pianos and reed organs. In addition he did repairs and rebuilt old instruments. Still feeling his way financially, he lived over the shop. Like everyone else, he met difficulties during the first world war but overcame them to the extent that two new factories were bought in London.

The company came to Doncaster in 1924, with the opening of a shop in Frenchgate. Gramophones and records were becoming an important section of the business at the time. This, together with the Depression in the thirties meant that very few pianos were in demand. Doncaster was one of three towns where retail shops continued business. When crystal radio sets were invented they very quickly became popular. Nevertheless it was necessary during the second war to re-organise the company under managing director J Raymond Fox. Charles Fox died at this time, leaving a very young son. After re-organisation the business consisted of the retail shop in Doncaster, together with some residential property in London which was later bombed.

For a while, trade in Doncaster depended on radiograms and television, but as interest in music revived in the fifties the shop concentrated again on keyboards and records. An attachment to the piano, known as the Selmer Clavioline, later developed into the electronic organ. It became popular in working men's clubs and also in churches.

Obtaining the Hammond organ agency was a turning point in the company's prosperity.

When a separate Organ Company was formed to market keyboards, the old television workshops in Coopers Terrace were converted into offices and sold to Marks & Spencers Ltd. The capital raised was used to open a keyboard centre in Nether Hall Road and a large record shop in the new Arndale Centre. At this point the managing Director's son David joined the business.

In 1974 a new Teaching Studio was opened in Doncaster. There was no age limit for classes which ranged from beginner level to advanced stages. The Studio, which is situated on Coopers Terrace, Doncaster, under the auspices of Yamaha, is managed by Kathy Eales for the teaching of guitar and piano.

The Company now has a prestigious store in the Meadowhall Shopping Centre, as well as branches in Nottingham, Leeds, Hull, Lincoln and Barnsley. Last year, the company was, again, Yamaha's largest independent dealer in the country and so the family tradition continues, with the hope that it will flourish for the younger generation of the family.

Below: *Frenchgate Organs 1988*
Top left: *Charles J Fox, the founder.*
Above: *An advertisement featuring delivery vehicles in 1918 and 1978.*
Above left: *An earlier version of the Frenchgate outlet.*

On the move

The volume of traffic entering and leaving French Gate to and from North Bridge and Trafford Street in this picture is typical of the problems faced by town planners all over the country in the 1960s. Doncaster was no exception and in this particular part of the town there was even greater urgency as this was the main road leading to the major towns and cities of the region. Brough's the grocers have by this time extended into Tom Smith's and followed the growing trend of becoming a self service shop. Jackson's is still standing before it is swallowed up by the Trafford Street/North Bridge development. The 1920s style architecture above the shops compares very favourably with the mock Tudor above Manfield shoe shop.

GOODLYS
GOODLYS
CABINETS
REGAL
BALBY
369
CDT 312

This takes a look at French Gate from the St. Sepulchre Gate end towards North Bridge. The trolley buses, both signed Balby, are probably making their way from the old trolley bus depot near North Bridge to the stop near the old Co-op where the Balby buses began their journey. Buses acquired Doncaster Corporation livery in 1956 although that was not the start of the trolley bus era. The last official bus ran on 14th December 1963. Goodly's Furniture and Cabinet makers had as its neighbour the Regal Cinema, which was known not without a great deal of affection as the 'flea pit'. This early 1960s photograph has not the same congestion of traffic that French Gate was to experience very quickly later and that was probably a good thing considering what hold-ups the roadroller could have caused.

A 630
A1
A60
BECKETT RD

The imposing portico at the entrance to the borough police headquarters of the Guildhall dominates this photograph with the clock at the junction with Baxter Gate towering over the locality. The importance of French Gate as a thoroughfare can be seen on the road sign. The A1, the country's main north-south route; A60 to Worksop and Mansfield; A630 to Rotherham. The advertisements just beyond the White Hart public house will bring back memories - the man of mystery associated with Sandeman's Port; the American influence of Three Three cigarettes from State Express and the well-known slogan of 'Players Please'. This side of the street was soon to make way for Arndale Centre, British Home Stores and C&A.

The tradition of St. Sepulchre Gate being the centre of the grocery business as well as the Mecca for people wanting to buy clothes and shoes is well illustrated in this 1950s photograph. Blakes, having its annual sale, was the place to purchase ladies and baby wear although its speciality was as a milliner. Trueform was then an independent shoeseller unlike today when the name of the shop is the only thing that is unique to it. The name Weaver to Wearer tries to tell its own story of the authenticity of its clothing and other shops in the same line here are Stylo Boot Company, Lucille Gowns, Dewhirst butchers and Willows outfitters before we reach the famous Hodgson and Hepworth. The trolley bus stand managed to outlast the shops and the spot continued to be the terminus long after these shops had disappeared.

FORM
BLAKES
ACE COURSE
SALE
SALE
SALE
377
CDT 638

Above: The principal purpose of Trafford Street when it was built in 1909/10 was to give direct access to the railway station from North Bridge. Another was to relieve the congestion at Clock Corner and St. Sepulchre Gate. Then in the 1920s it became the town centre terminus for trams on the Brodsworth and Bentley routes and the introduction of trolley buses in the 1930s meant that this street took on an even more important role in the traffic life of the town. In 1951 it was recognised by the corporation that the town's traffic difficulties were two-fold. The first was the amount of through traffic using the High Street, French Gate, Trafford Street, North Bridge route and also from local traffic in the area. This photograph taken at the time is a good example of the problem, although the lady pedestrian seems quite oblivious to the cars, vans and lorries. The solution was the provision of an inner ring road to divert traffic away from the town centre and Trafford Street became Trafford Way, a dual 33 feet carriageway with a central reservation although it took another ten years before it was reconsidered and a modified plan came to fruition in 1969 without the planned fly-over at the French Gate end of the street.

Veteran vintage and modern car doctors to the north of England

Two brothers, Eddie and Robert Arnett, set up their motor vehicle repair business in Cleveland Street, Doncaster in 1946. Robert had had previous experience working for Bernard Cutriss Ltd as his foreman when the brothers bought the engineering part of the Cutriss business.

Robert took charge of the engineering whilst Eddie was the firm's administrator. The firm generated its own electricity and used old lineshaft machines to begin with but modernising was soon begun when funds became available.

The firm remained at its first premises until 1955. Then the site was required for the old ABC cinema complex and the Arnetts' business moved to Bentink Street. There was a further move in 1969, this time to purpose-built premises which were designed to house the latest automobile engine technology the business was using.

The firm's work is mainly local but they specialise in maintaining and repairing vintage engines in the vehicles owned throughout the north of England.

Their customers are chiefly the main vehicle agents in the Doncaster area but they also serve a good many small garages, private individuals and enthusiasts, providing re-manufactured and repaired engines and parts at competitive costs. The work is done by a skilled team led by a degree-holding director.

The company's aim is to develop its ability to cope with increasingly complex engines. It seems that they are succeeding since Mr Arnett says, 'People keep telling us that we can do the impossible.'

Above: *Some of the complex-looking equipment used at the Arnetts' second premises between 1955 and 1969.*
Left: *The purpose-built premises that Arnetts currently occupy, the picture taken in 1969.*
Below: *One of the vintage cars serviced by Arnetts, a Bullnose Cowley from about 1930.*

A 'sit-in' brings Ford to Doncaster

Charlesworths' motor car business was established by Edgar Charlesworth at Wombwell near Barnsley during 1913. To embark on this venture, eighteen year old Edgar left an engineering course at Sheffield University. This was a time when the motor trade was beginning to expand and Edgar thought that he would try to find a niche in this business rather than follow his university studies.

A year later Edgar was called up to join the army. leaving his father, an insurance salesman, to run the motor business. Before long, Edgar was invalided out of the army with tuberculosis and, after that, father and son formed the motor company E & G Charlesworth.

By 1918 the business was retailing Ford cars for a Leeds company owned by Roland Winn who had a Ford franchise. Two years later, Charlesworths tried to obtain their own franchise but Ford turned them down.

George Charlesworth was not a man to be content with a polite rebuff. He staged a one-man sit in at the Ford plant at Trafford Park, Manchester. After four days, Ford relented, realising that if he was so keen to get his franchise, then his enthusiasm would fuel his keenness to sell cars.

During the early twenties the company prospered. As well as increasing their vehicle, tractor and spare parts sales, it became the major local repairer of Model T Ford cars and a fitter of 'tipping gear' for trucks. The Wombwell workshop, accommodating in the region of ten mechanics, was an old aeroplane hangar which had been bought from a sale of government surplus stock at Beverley. It was transported to Wombwell by canal and to move it from the waterside to the Charlesworth site a Fordson tractor and Model T trucks were used.

Edgar and George were involved in several entrepreneurial projects, including one of the first bus services between Wombwell and Barnsley which was operated by Edgar himself. By 1925 the firm was ripe for further expansion and a site was bought at Bennetthorpe, Doncaster which the company occupied in 1926. Edgar and his new wife Hilda from the midlands concentrated on the new business whilst George wound down operations at Wombwell, leaving there in 1928.

Then George too moved to Doncaster to assist his son in the firm's fight for a proportion of the town's motor trade. Their main competition during the twenties and thirties came from E.W. Jackson in

Above: *The original premises, Barnsley Road, Wombwell.*
Left: *Edgar Charlesworth sitting in the 250,00th British Ford in 1926.*
Below: *The workshops at Bennetthorpe.*

French Gate, W.E. Clark & Company in Station Road and Claybourns in Waterdale.

During the Second World War, Charlesworths were registered under the Ministry of Supply to carry out essential repairs to vehicles that were specifically needed in the war effort. This involved a lot of work on tractors and other agricultural machinery. Government regulations restricted the number of cars that could be sold and priority was given to doctors and other workers whose journeys were, as the posters demanded, 'really necessary'.

In spite of a post-war shortage of materials, Charlesworths'' business increased and it soon became clear that more spacious premises were needed. The firm acquired a 2.25 acre site at Barnby Dun Road, Doncaster. The existing buildings on it had housed tractors and agricultural implements but Charlesworths concentrated here on the sale and repair of trucks. Later the Barnby Dun site would accommodate a used-car display area, paint and body shop and parts department.

In the early fifties, Edgar's daughter and only child, Christiana, joined the firm. Educated at Doncaster Girls' High School and Oxford University, she had

Above: *The Charlesworth staff outside the Bennetthorpe premises in the early years. Edgar Charlesworth is extreme right. George is on the front row, left of the gentleman in the bowler hat.*

Below: *Amy Johnson drove a Ford V8 in the pre-war Monte Carlo Rally. She is seen here (centre front) at the Doncaster checkpoint with her co-driver, Mrs McAvoy, an RAC official, Edgar Charlesworth and some of his employees.*

Left: *A Ford pick-up truck brings in a job.*
Bottom: *During the Second World War at Bennetthorpe. There were no cars to display during wartime and so the windows were filled with exhibitions of wartime activities.*
Below: *A line-up of vehicles in the Bennetthorpe workshop in 1927.*

worked in London for the Rank Organisation but the family persuaded her to return to Doncaster to handle Charlesworths' publicity and promotional work. New Ford cars she promoted during the 50s included the Consul, Anglia and Cortina which all became immensely popular. They are much sought after today as collectors' items.
In 1954, George Charlesworth died aged 83. He had lived in Victoria Crescent and despite his close involvement with the motor industry had found time to be an active Rotarian, travelling with the association to Austria and the United States. Christiana left the company temporarily in 1957 in order to bring up her family. Meanwhile, Edgar planned to modernise the Bennetthorpe site. By 1963,

alongside many other new developments in Doncaster, Charlesworths presented a new and modern face to the motor trade. The rebuilt premises included new showroom extensions, service, reception and administration areas.

Within a year of the completion of all this modernisation, Edgar Charlesworth died aged 68. He had been at the helm of a business which had started humbly in Wombwell at the dawn of the age of the motor car. He died knowing his firm was prosperous, revitalised and ready to compete in the 1960s boom. Edgar's death was mourned not only in the Doncaster motor industry but also by other sections of the community. He had been Chairman of the Doncaster Chamber of Commerce and a director of Doncaster Rovers Football team. He had received an MBE and a CBE for his work with the National Savings movement.

His successor as managing director of the firm was Charles Heeks, who had started with Charlesworths as an apprentice in Wombwell when there were only eight employees. He was now in charge of a workforce of over 100. Four years later, Christiana returned to the company as his deputy, taking over sole charge at Mr Heeks' death in 1976. During her ten year term of office Charlesworths continued to update its facilities and offer the Ford Motor Company's wide range of cars.

The company is currently run by Mr Tony Charlesworth, Christiana's son by her first marriage who has adopted his maternal grandfather's name. He is Doncaster born and worked for some time with Fords at Brentwood before returning home to take charge of the family business.

Above: *The early 1950s. A reminder of the years when Ford cars were manufactured in Doncaster.*
Below: *The Bennetthorpe showroom pictured in the 1960s.*

For journeys near and far

Wilfreda Luxury Coaches Limited was established in 1949. Mr. W.G. S. Scholey purchased one coach from Wilfred Graham who in 1948 had bought a coach to enhance his already thriving taxi business which he ran alongside his other business Restholme Transport Cafe in Bawtry. He had named the coach after his daughter Wilfreda Jean and Bill Scholey decided to retain this unusual name.

After selling their business the 'Grahams' emigrated to Australia and Wilfreda Jean now lives in Brisbane. During Wilf's lifetime in Australia he was always very interested in the well being of the Company and followed its progress over the years.

Bill and Marie Scholey ran Wilfreda Coaches alongside their Quarry and Haulage business from 1949 to 1978 together with their family, Tony, Paul and Pene. During the 50's and early 60's the coaching business thrived as people wanted to visit places of interest which after World War 11 were now accessible once again and a day to the seaside by coach was a special treat. New coaches were purchased on a regular basis either from Plaxtons at Scarborough or Duples in London and latterly their factory in Blackpool.

The late 60's and early 70's saw the age of the car and people became more prosperous, better housing and roads were needed to meet public demand. The family concentrated all their efforts on the quarry business during this building boom . The coaching business at this time became somewhat of a side line.

In 1976 Sue Scholey joined the Company and together with Tony started to re-build the Company. New tenders were sought and won with the National Coal Board, Central Electricity Board, Schools and Colleges. Bill and Marie Scholey were always on hand for advice during their retirement years and on their death were sadly missed by all the family and many friends they made during their business years.

The next decade was a time of change. The business was growing rapidly. Passengers were demanding more out of coach travel as motorways made travelling by coach faster and more comfortable. Wilfreda were one of the first operators in the area to serve coffee and tea whilst travelling. This facility was much appreciated by their following of regular passengers.

Tony and Sue operated a small tour programme and many holidays were enjoyed by their regular customers, Tony drove the coach and Sue looked after the passengers often helped by their very young son Peter who travelled many miles in his specially adapted 'car seat'.

Difficult times were experienced during the long miners strike, contracts were on hold for 12 months and times were hard for all in the area. Not to be deterred Wilfreda carried on with her normal enthusiasm and the Company opened an office on Bawtry High Street to promote the Tour, Excursion and Private hire programme. Having this good position in Bawtry drew the public's attention and proved to be a very successful venture.

Due to the Company's steady growth the premises in Bawtry were becoming too cramped at this time Beehive Services in Doncaster was on the market. The Directors sought advice and it was decided

Above: *The first new vehicle bought by Mr Scholey, a Foden Coach chassis with 33 seater Windover Body. It was purchased from Beeches Garage, Stoke-on-Trent.* ***Left:*** *A Bedford VAL chassis with Duple body built at Hendon. This vehicle was purchased in 1962.*

to go for further rapid expansion by acquiring Beehive together with all it's employees.
By this time both Sue's older sons Phil and Nigel, had joined the Company. Phil trained as a PCV Driver and took over the Tour programme, later to become Sales and Operations Manager. While Nigel trained as a PCV mechanic at Tile Hill College in Coventry. In January 1988 Wilfreda and Beehive moved from Bawtry to Adwick-le-Street to larger premises. Originally this garage was the home of Kildare Coaches and is ideally located for easy access to the motorway network.
It was becoming more and more apparent at this time that there was to be a very rapid decline in contract work due to the demise of the coal industry. To address this challenge and to give the Company and its workforce stability in the future, stage carriage bus service was to be the next venture. This started by tendering for subsidised services administered by South Yorkshire Transport Executive who after deregulation became responsible for providing a network of services in South Yorkshire which were not commercially viable but were socially necessary. Over the next few years a network of services evolved in competition with other local operators in Doncaster, Barnsley and Sheffield. 1993 saw the acquisition of Roeville Tours another old established Company in the area. From November, 1995 this Company operates the Taxi business from the same premises with 'London' style cabs which were purchased new from LTI in London to give Doncaster good old fashioned service backed up by new vehicles and professional uniformed drivers.
The Company had now over a relatively short period heavily invested in vehicles purchasing eight new Scanias and an Executive Bova in '89 to enhance tour and private hire.
In 1992 eight new Dennis Darts were acquired to update the ageing bus fleet. The Bova has proved to be an ideal vehicle for Tours and private hire and was added to the fleet each year.

In 1997, to enable the Company to concentrate on its original core business the stage carriage business was disposed of to Mainline who now have consolidated all routes into their own network.
Investment in rolling stock has always been a priority with Wilfreda and through her colourful history many different vehicles have been operated. There have been many changes but some things do not. Wilfreda Beehive is still a family business and may the next generation add a few more chapters to her memoirs.

Above: *An early bus, a Bedford used by the company in the 1950s.* ***Top:*** *Whether these avid football fans are coming from or going to the match is unclear but the mood of excitement is evident. The staff of Beehive were clearly caught up in the atmosphere.* ***Left:*** *Part of the new fleet of luxury coaches with the distinctive Wilfreda Beehive logo on the front.*

The company that introduced the East to the West

The F. Cross & Sons group of motor dealers is one of Britain's most remarkable automotive success stories of the 1990s, but their story really begins over forty years ago in 1958. That was the year that Fred and Peggy Cross purchased a four-acre site at Hatfield on the outskirts of Doncaster. Fred had previously carried out car repairs in a small workshop in Stainforth. The new site consisted of just three petrol pumps and a modest workshop and offered a service of car repairs, car sales and fuel. The garage was situated on the A1146 on the outskirts of Hatfield. This was a busy road carrying the Doncaster-to-east coast traffic.

The early days

The Cross family did well and in 1962 a small showroom was built. It housed used cars, together with a few new Fords and Austins for supply to established customers. More customers were turning to Fred Cross for their new cars but an attempt to obtain a new-car franchise was unsuccessful because all the established franchises were taken.

A family concern

In 1964, Fred and Peggy's son, Peter Cross joined the business after serving an apprenticeship in radio/television servicing. The same year, his brother, Ronnie joined straight from school.

Two years later in 1966 the Cross family took the far-sighted decision to become dealers for a car marque that was widely respected in the far east but virtually unknown in the UK. An advertisement had appeared in the national press

for new dealers to sell Toyota, an unknown Japanese car at the time.

The turning point

The family made enquiries and inspected one model Corona 1500. They were so impressed with the quality, build and engineering of this model that they took a calculated risk. They became a Toyota franchise. The Toyota Corona appeared in the Cross family's small showroom from June to December that year and 18 were sold. When, in 1972 a second model was added to the range, Mr Cross invested in new showrooms and service facilities, including a 6,000 square foot workshop which is the only original building left today.

Above: *The old Garage on the A1146 in 1972. A rather impressive new Daimler from Mr Cross' stock overshadows the other vehicles line up behind.*
Left: *A Toyota Corona on display on the forecourt is an original. A sticker on its front passenger door celebrates 30 years as a Toyota dealership. It is interesting to note the changes that the Toyota range has undergone over the years although die-hard fans will look at this model and mourn its passing.*

"IN 1966, THE CROSS FAMILY TOOK THE DECISION TO BECOME DEALERS FOR AN UNKNOWN RANGE OF JAPANESE CARS. THAT RANGE WAS TOYOTA."

family business being marooned in a cul-de-sac.

Protests and objections were made to no avail and in 1977 the worst happened, or so it was thought at the time. However, such was the reputation built up in the town by F Cross and Sons that the business did not fade and die.

Further expansion

In fact, the partnership between the Cross family and Toyota proved to be so rewarding that in 1989 their company expanded once again by making a major investment in new, modern Toyota showroom, service and bodyshop departments at Hatfield.

The year after was a double success, bringing F Cross and Sons a franchise from Lexus and a success for their sales team in winning the coveted National Sales Guild Award for vehicle sales and professionalism.

The company has an almost-40-year association with Toyota and have established an excellent reputation for sales and service.

In the mid-seventies rumours were heard about a new motorway, the M18. The Cross family realised that, if it went ahead, it would result in the A114 being blocked off and and the Cross

The company has a unique approach to sales. Each sales executive is fully trained by Toyota so that he/she knows every feature of their entire range. A full demonstrator fleet is at the

Above: *Fred and Peggy Cross, founders of the company.*
Right: *F. Cross & Sons is the oldest established Authorised Toyota Dealer in England, Scotland and Wales. The company's sales team recently won the coveted National Sales Guild Award for profession-alism, making them the number one Toyota dealership in the United Kingdom.*

customer's disposal and test drives are offered not only from the company's premises but also from the customer's home or office. A computerised product-finding facility helps the company find the right vehicle for each customer.

In 1972 the former Bates Garage was acquired by F. Cross & Sons. In 1987 the family invested £1 million in transforming the garage into a 30 vehicle showroom with an integral five bay service department, changing the name to Chaceside.

In 1990 the company was awarded the prestigious Lexus franchise, whilst in 1991 the sales team won the coveted National Sales Guild Award for vehicle sales and professionalism, making them the number one Toyota dealership in the UK. In the same year, the company made a successful bid to become an authorised Volkswagon/Audi franchise dealer.

Taking over an existing dealership in Scunthorpe represented a £1.5 million investment for them and was their first acquisition in a strategic five year growth plan. When, in 1992, the Volkswagon Golf won the European Car of the Year Award it helped to give the new dealership the image of quality that F. Cross & Company wanted to project in Scunthorpe.

"THE COMPANY NOW HAS AN ALMOST 40 YEAR ASSOCIATION WITH TOYOTA WITH RELATIVE NEWCOMERS BEING KIA AND LEXUS."

F. Cross & Sons strengthened their relationship with Toyota as the Carina E and Corolla models were launched in 1992 and the Toyota Supra in 1993.

The Chaceside garage was transformed again in 1992 into a modern new Kia franchise. To support the launch of the new Kia the group invested in new showrooms, fully equipped service facilities and expertly trained technicians. The company takes great pride in having introduced Kia to the region.

Above: *Mr Peter Cross demonstrates Toyota's flourishing business in Doncaster to a representative of the Japanese company that F. Cross helped to introduce to Great Britain.*

At work

The beginnings of the construction of a new police station and law courts across from the Waterdale complex show the scale of redevelopment in the area. This was the original site of Tattersall's yearling sales, known as Glasgow Grounds or Paddocks. The contrast between old and new can be seen as we look at the modern buildings in the centre with the terraced houses beginning with Honor Bright's newsagents on the left up from the Waterdale complex. The original plans for the Golden Acres was intended to cover the area on the top left bounded by Spring Gardens (now College Road), Waterdale, Wood Street and Cleveland Street and demolition did occur. The old bus station is still functioning at this time with buses bound for Sheffield, Edlington, Tickhill and Worksop waiting to leave. At the top of the photograph stands the solitary spire of Christ Church.

The redevelopment of the area across from Waterdale now includes the Doncaster College, Teachers' Centre, Police Station and Law Courts. Glasgow Paddocks,which takes up most of that land held its last Tattersalls sale there in 1957. During the Second World War part of this area was utilised as a bus station and this continued for some time afterwards until 1968 when the Southern Bus Station was built. Originally the plans for this part of Doncaster included a new Town Hall, technical college, museum and art gallery, library as well as police station and law courts and a pedestrian way rather than a main road. The new Town Hall in a later plan was to have a ten-storey tower. In the end as with the nearby Golden Acres all the plans were never carried out and the whole area has an air of being under-developed.

Picture: Sheffield Newspapers Ltd

Above: The redevelopment of the corner of St. Sepulchre Gate and French Gate was announced to the public of Doncaster in the Doncaster Chronicle in February 1962 and the businesses destined to make way for the new centre were being acquired by the development company, Arndale Property Trust Limited. The demise of the small local businessman was well prophesied at the time as it was felt they would not be able to afford the high rents the developers were intending to charge and this would only make way for nationally established businesses which had the wherewithal to be able to afford the outlay necessary. The well established landmarks of Doncaster like Clock Corner, the Midland Bank building with its distinctive roof and dome, and the just visible rounded corner of the Royal Buildings which housed the Blackburn Assurance Company above Timpson's shoes stand in complete contrast with the demolition of the opposite corner.

Below: The pram may be of uncertain age as might be the Gestetner duplicator, an office essential prior to the advent of the photocopier, but the photograph is accurately dated to August 1965 when this part of Doncaster was demolished to make way for the Waterdales Shopping Centre, originally known as the Golden Acres. The developers claimed it would be the finest shopping centre in Europe. No redevelopment ever pleases everyone nor does it not cause a few ripples. In this case it was more than a ripple. The original plans were accused of driving industry out of the part of Doncaster that needed it most. Then the plans were watered down. As the project progressed, some more of the proposals were changed and on completion of the development, there was great difficulty in the letting of shops as the world-wide recession hit Doncaster. The town council meeting in March 1967 ended in fierce arguments and the thriving business community envisaged for this area was slow to get off the ground.

Brook Crompton - a place in the history of electrical engineering

In 1878 when electric street lighting was first introduced in London, Yorkshireman Colonel Crompton, a pioneer of the electrical industry, established RE Crompton & Company in Chelmsford. In it's first year the company provided a lighting system for a new foundry in Derbyshire and then proceeded to work towards developing alternative electrical systems, including electric motors, cooking and heating appliances and traction equipment.

In 1927 Crompton and Company amalgamated with the Yorkshire firm F & A.E. Parkinson Ltd to form Crompton Parkinson, becoming a major supplier of electric motors in this country and an internationally recognised player in the market.

Following this merger, the company began to implement long flow production line methods and use more sophisticated precision tools, utilising F & A.E Parkinson's key manufacturing skills. Seventy years on, long flow production lines have been replaced by a modern cell manufacturing practice. The company now uses highly sophisticated CNC machine tools and a modern computerised system to design and produce a wide range of motors.

Left: *Colonel R.E.B. Crompton, one of the founders of the company and a pioneer in electrical science.*
Below: *Final assembly. A line of workers assembling the components to make complete motors.*

It was in 1940 that Crompton Parkinson first moved to Doncaster, to operate a factory for the manufacture of small arms ammunition for the Ministry of Supply. The Doncaster site was a suitable place for this purpose, as there was plenty of room for expansion and a surplus of labour locally available to work in

Above: *Hand insertion of coils, before machine insertion became standard practice.* ***Left:*** *Dynamometer testing of motors in the 1950s.*

Above: *Motor packing in the 1950s. Although still labour intensive, multi-pack cartons are now more commonly used.*
Left: *An early winding machine.*

the factory. After the war Crompton Parkinson purchased another 32 acres of land to increase the company's production.

Brook Crompton Parkinson Motors was formed in 1974 by merging Brook Motors Ltd with the electric motor interests of Crompton Parkinson, both of which were part of the Hawker Siddeley Group. The resulting new company became the market leader in low voltage ac electric motors. A new product, the M20 was launched in 1984, which was particularly suitable for the growing shower and beer pump, office machinery and DIY markets.

In 1990 the fractional motor factory at Newcastle-Under-Lyme was acquired from leading competitor GEC Electromotors. Following the BTR takeover of Hawker Siddeley in 1991, the Newcastle plant was transferred to the Doncaster site, where the company is now part of BTR's large Power Drives group. This provided a major challenge to the Doncaster business, as the Newcastle-under-Lyme facility needed integrating into the Doncaster site, which involved the transfer of over 500 machines and an increase in the workforce.

Nowadays the company's main market sectors for which motors are produced include, heating, ventilation and air-conditioning, pumps, business machines, food processing equipment and general mechanical drives. The bulk of the products are sold in the UK and exported into mainland Europe.

Above: *The company prepares to expand.*
Below: *an aerial view of the company site and its surrounding area.*

Plumbing excellence to the four corners of the earth

The two founders of Pegler were born in Doncaster but met each other in Glasgow. Frank Pegler had developed a merchant business there where he made contact with brass-founders McKay for whom Birchall worked.

On December 1st 1899 the firm that the pair founded began in a very humble way with a handful of workers in a two storey building in North Union Street. The rent was £50 a year and Mr Fred Birchall, with the help of just one man, personally occupied himself with fitting up and equipping the workshop.

The first 25 horse power gas engine started up in March 1900, the day Ladysmith was relieved, and a moulder, a core maker and a brass finisher were engaged. The Doncaster foundry was engaged mainly to make products for the steam industry which were sold through the merch-anting company,

Above left: Fred Birchall and Frank Pegler were both local men who met in Glasgow and later founded the company.
Above: The erection of the 200ft Pegler chimney at Belmont works, Balby in 1932 meant Doncaster had a new landmark.
Below: A charming office scene from the 1930s from long before the days of high-tech computers

Pegler Bros & Co. At this period a skilled man was paid about 32s (£1.50) a week and a boy 4s (20p).

Fred was joined by his brother Andrew, a pattern maker and at the end of 1900 there was a work force of 70. By 1903 the company had a debt of £3,600 and planned to move to larger premises in order to increase production and so get into profit. Land was purchased at Balby and in 1904 Belmont Works was built. It was just a mile from the centre of Doncaster, easily travelled by the expanding workforce.

A trip to the United States by Fred Birchall in 1913 resulted in the pneumatic chuck being introduced into the factory as well as capstan lathes.

When war was declared the company became registered as a private limited company under the name Pegler Brothers & Company (Doncaster) Ltd. There were 195 employees, 14 of them women. During the war the company was controlled by the government to make brass, iron and steel fuses for munitions. An aircraft shop was erected in 1917 and by the end of the war the first Sopwith-Camels were coming off the assembly.

At the end of the war the factory resumed its production of water fittings. steam and radiator valves. Chromium plating was introduced. Much trade had gone to competitors who had not been on munitions but the postwar boom made room for them all. Steam power was replaced with gas and oil engines and then electricity. Pegler were pioneers in installing first an extruding press, then a stamping press, helping the company to weather the difficult times of the General Strike.

Above: *The assembly of gas valves in the 1960s. Beehive hairstyles and pale faces prompted by the likes of Jean Shrimpton and Lulu were becoming popular.*
Left: *A dramatic advertising promotion from around the same period. It would be very difficult for most Doncaster people to imagine their town without this familiar landmark.*

In 1932 the company name was changed to Peglers Ltd. and shortly afterwards Doncaster acquired a new landmark with the erection of a 200 foot chimney.

In the second war the aircraft carrier Ark Royal was fitted with 6,000 Pegler non-concussive taps, whilst more than 2,000 employees fulfilled sub-contracts for Rolls Royce, Vickers Armstrong and British Thermostat.

The factory was mechanised in 1946 with the high-tech of the day and peacetime production was geared to rebuilding. The following year Fred Birchall retired at the age of 77! Then the recession of the 50s hit Pegler. There was a shortage of copper and there were redundancies and short time.

The first orders for small bore radiator valves were received in 1962 and Pegler went on to lead the world with these products. Mason Brothers of Dewsbury were bought out and all of the senior managers in the countrywide service depots had learned their trade in Doncaster.

As far back as 1927 Pegler had an agent in Denmark and today they sell to more than 100 countries worldwide. In 1968 Pegler Holdings Ltd as the company was known by then merged with Hattersley Holdings to form Pegler-Hattersley. This in turn was taken over by the midlands-based engineering and manufacturing conglomerate Tomkins Plc.

The company now has one of the most modern factories of its type in Europe and its manufacturing centre in Doncaster has been awarded the coveted British Standards Institute BS5750 Quality Assured Factory certification. To the customer this means a continuous superior standard in all aspects of production.

The Pegler commitment to investment is impressive. Over the past five years it has invested in its manufacturing facilities at an average rate of £3.5 million a year. Sales are at record levels.

Competitiveness is important to Pegler. They will never be the cheapest but they guarantee value for money from products that are fit for the purpose and backed by the company's total support package.

The ambition of Fred Birchall and the entrepreneurial spirit of Frank Pegler launched what is now one of the most go-ahead companies in South Yorkshire.

Above: *Girls working in the radiator valve assembly cell.*
Left: *A designer adding the finishing touches to a new kitchen tap.*

The estate agents with an edge on the competition

Estate agents C Barnsdale & Son set up their business in Copley Road, Doncaster about 90 years ago. At the time, Charles Barnsdale was managing the property affairs of the Flowitt family. The Flowitts were builders who had built many late 19th century Doncaster houses.

In the late 1920s Charles' son Frederick joined him and the business moved to larger premises in Nether Hall Road.

"UNTIL THE 1960S, MANY DONCASTER PEOPLE RENTED THEIR HOUSES - ONLY THE WELL-TO-DO BOUGHT."

Frederick's son Malcolm was born in 1941. As a boy he had helped his father out at weekends but he had made no decision to go into the family business when he went to study at Worksop College.

When the firm's rent collector died at Christmas 1960, however, Malcolm was due to finish at Worksop and started work in his place on January 1st 1960. There were few other staff. Malcolm's father Frederick carried out valuations and surveys. Charles his grandfather died in April 1961, proud and happy that the third generation had thrown in his lot with the firm.

For three days a week Malcolm collected rents from around a thousand properties in areas that included Balby, Hexthorpe, Bentley and Hyde Park. Three quarters of the firm's business was involved with property management.

Until the sixties in Doncaster many people rented property and only the well-to-do bought their own houses. Three years later Malcolm turned his attention to house sales.

In the early 70s, Malcolm's brother Frederick, usually known as Butch, joined the firm.

Presently the firm deals with the sale and purchase of all types of residential and commercial property and property management including rent collection within a ten mile radius of Doncaster. They also prepare inventories and valuations and supervise repairs. Commercial property matters are dealt with by Neal Craven, who joined the firm in 1986 and became a Partner in 1991. The Partnership was further expanded in 1997 with the acquisition of Norths Estate Agency of Hatfield and Thorne, thus adding two offices to the firm.

Jason and Matthew Barnsdale, the sons of Malcolm are bringing a fourth generation to the business as they finish their university courses. With the firm's ability to adapt to the present climate, the future looks as bright as its past.

Above: *The firm's founder, Charles Barnsdale.*
Left: *The office premises in 1906. This is how they remained until alterations were begun in September 1965.*

The company that began in a cow-shed

This company, well known in Doncaster for hydraulic cylinders, equipment and design, was set up in 1948 with a loan from the founder's grandfather. The first premises were a rented cowshed but this was no problem for the stout-hearted Howard Bishop. His grandfather had accrued the £400 in his grocery store in Hatfield High Street which later housed Boughons' butcher's shop.

Whilst the embryo business was gathering force to bring him in a salary Howard Bishop worked as a part time PT instructor. Nor did he try to save his energies for his business by choosing easy pupils. A reference from the governor of H.M. Borstal Institution described the lads he instructed as 'ranging from the under-privileged to the over-indulged; from the victim of circumstances to the hardened young delinquent' and his achievement with them was to 'infuse a keenness for his subject and a most satisfactory standard of attainment.'

Above: ***Above:** Hatfield Carnival in 1923. The procession passes Mr Bishop's premises. The groom in the procession (bottom right) is Robert Baker, father of Janet Baker the opera singer, together with his 'bride' Stanley Fidler.*
***Top:** Hatfield High Street. Mr Bishop had a grocery store shown extreme right which later became Boughons' butcher's shop. The ground floor of the parochial institute was taken over by the London, City and Midland Bank in 1909. The top floor was later occupied by the public library until a new library was opened in 1974.*
***Right:** A Gullicks' lorry picking up mining machinery from outside the Dunscroft site.*

A by-product of Mr Bishop's inventive mind was his 'Boomerang' of which he is justly proud. The idea behind it is simple and effective. A ball is slung on a piece of string hanging from an overhead crossbar. When it is struck, it flies forward, curls under a metal sheet and comes straight back to the batsman, on a good length every time. It gained the approval of the Australian all-rounder who was the scourge of many an English test team in the fifties.

As was to be expected, this Doncaster all-rounder soon progressed in his business life out of his cowshed into a stable, which he purchased in 1951 and which sufficed him until he could afford his

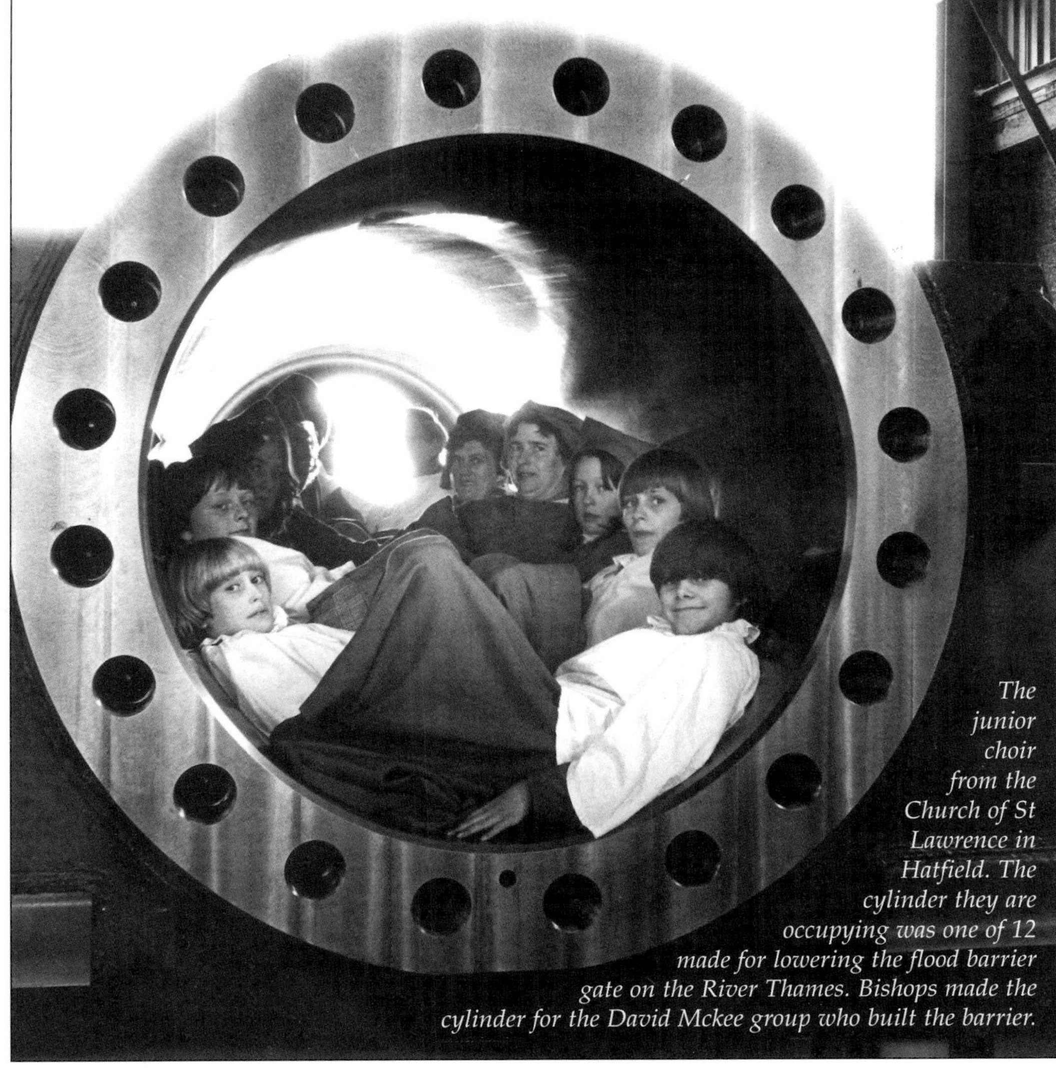

The junior choir from the Church of St Lawrence in Hatfield. The cylinder they are occupying was one of 12 made for lowering the flood barrier gate on the River Thames. Bishops made the cylinder for the David Mckee group who built the barrier.

present, purpose-built premises on Bootham Lane, Dunscroft, in 1963.

His company provides an engineering service to the automobile, mining and hydraulics industries and the workers are pioneers in special precision techniques. Machines have been developed over the years to produce the finest quality cylinders in ferrous and non ferrous metals for a wide variety of applications.

The factory has a production area of 23,000 square feet. There is a range of conventional metal cutting machines together with a variety of specialist tools manned by a skilled work force. The company is manufacturer to the nuclear, paper-making, oilfield, mining and chemical industries.

In 1990, after completing an order for a Scipio Launch tube for Rocket Motors Division of Royal Ordnance plc, the company became included in the Rocket Motors Division register of suppliers

Their proud boast is, 'We know of no other company with such a wide range of cylinder-making and testing facilities and our dedicated staff pride themselves in a quality product at a competitive price.' The company is sure that orders will continue to pour in when it expands into its new factory expansion in 1998.

Below: *A closer look at the dunscroft site from November 1963.*

The sweet story of success

It was a lucky break for Doncaster when Giovanni Massarella and his brother Dominic decided to build new lives for their families in England instead of continuing their journey to America in 1860.

Giovanni settled in Doncaster and Dominic made his home in Leicester and they both started to make and sell ice cream in 1861, building their own handcarts.

In time, Giovanni's four sons - Carmine, Lewis, Vincente and Andrew - started independent ice cream businesses and also developed smallholdings. Andrew later trained many international showjumpers including Mister Softee and his sons John and Andrew junior represented Great Britain.

In 1945, all the branches of the family pooled resources and combined with the ice cream firms of relatives Rebori and Co (Rotherham) and J Carolis (Sheffield) to form Massarella Supplies Ltd.

The original family home was Belmont House in Cooke Street (now Church Street), Bentley. Massarella's then purchased a 10 acre site north of Jossey Lane on the Great North Road and a former skating rink on Hunt Lane. This rink had been requisitioned by the army during the war and was developed by Massarellas into the most advanced and largest ice cream factory in Europe at that time.

Ice cream was being produced in bulk by 1949 and by 1954 a fleet of refrigerated vans served three depots in Doncaster and others in Sheffield, Rotherham, Scunthorpe, Wakefield, Driffield, Leicester and Coalville. From these, 300 closed vans covered the country from Darlington to Coventry.

Above: *The family as seen in the late 1920s, with the current Chairman, Ronnie Massarella far right, as a young boy.*

Left: *Richard Massarella as a young man standing proudly beside an early ice-cream van, charmingly named after Irene, Ronnie's sister.*

During 1950s, health inspectors from around the country and America visited and stood in awe at the production processes and advanced hygiene and safety devices and procedures in the Bentley factory.

The business was then sold to J Lyons and in 1963 Ronnie Massarella and his cousin Andrew junior repurchased a part of the retail side of the company. Andrew junior then managed the business in Doncaster.

The Belmont House factory, which still carries the family name as Allied Massarella (Ice Cream Direct) is now owned by David Dimon who joined the former Massarella Company in 1959 as a part-time driver, with his wife, Hazel working full-time. This is now a sales and distribution depot for Nestle/Treats and Walls ice cream products while the Massarellas have moved into the wider fields of catering and farming.

There are now over 100 operations within the Massarella Catering Group which has restaurants in major departmental stores nationwide as well as in shopping centres including Meadowhall, the Alhambra Centre (Barnsley), the Victoria Centre (Nottingham), the Shires (Leicester), the Metro Centre (Gateshead) and Lakeside, (Thurrock).

When Giovanni and Dominic left Settefati, near Cassino, all those years ago they could never have envisaged that Giovanni's great-grandsons - Mark, Jeremy, Michael and Stephen - would now be in day to day control of a multi-million pounds company or that in the 1990s Giovanni's grandson, Ronnie, would be Chairman of the Massarella Catering Group and Chef d'Equipe the British Olympic Showjumping Team.

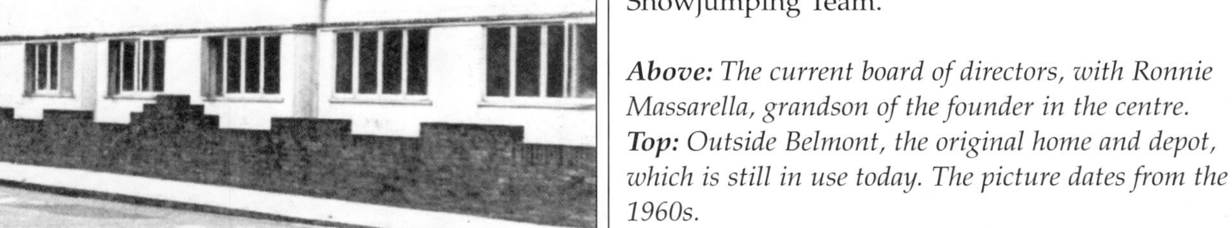

***Above:** The current board of directors, with Ronnie Massarella, grandson of the founder in the centre.*
***Top:** Outside Belmont, the original home and depot, which is still in use today. The picture dates from the 1960s.*
***Left:** The Hunt Lane Factory.*

R.E. Trem - the company with the personal touch

After his war service in the RAF, Mr R E Trem operated for a time as a private individual trader. Enquiries from abroad for engines and engineering parts sent him to the Ministry of War and the Ministry of Supply where he could obtain them. Realising that here was a niche in the market that he could fill, he set up a business in Doncaster in 1947 dealing in surplus military equipment, commercial vehicles and spare parts such as fishing trawler engine units and small diesel electric generating sets.

After five years in Doncaster, the business moved to Old Bawtry Road, Finningley which is still the company site. Things went well here and in 1973 a purpose-built warehouse of 10,000 square feet was erected.

In 1981 Mr D E Trem joined the business, taking it into its second generation. Mr Trem senior operates sales and marketing and is chairman of the Board. His son operates production/Engineering and is the managing director.

The site now covers six acres and a further warehouse was built, this time with an eight thousand square feet capacity, in 1994, giving a total of over 24,000 square feet of covered workshop space.

Trems' customers are mostly small firms who are hoping to reduce their electrical energy costs by using self-powered generators and larger organisa-tions who have to have back-up supplies in case of a

failure in the public supply. Trems stock now includes very large diesel engine power units

The company receives much of its business from personal recommendation and makes minimal use of advertising, especially abroad. Machines and parts are exported worldwide with no particular country accounting for a majority of sales. The high quality refurbished equipment is often bought by shipping companies.

The firm attributes its popularity with its customers to its competitive prices and its speed of response to orders. It offers free technical advice from its wealth of experience in solving clients' problems.

Requests are received for manufacturing plant for such diverse purposes as oil-refining and hand soap production, this is when the company takes a personal interest in all its customers problems, and where necessary they supply an Installation Team and Service Engineers worldwide.

The firm's workforce is small and loyal, most having been with Trem for at least twenty years. The advantages of this are obvious but the danger is that they will all retire together, leaving the company without the expertise its customers rely on. To obviate this difficulty Trem has advertised over the last five years for younger people as trainees.

There are plans for the future which include diversification into new and possibly unrelated trade sectors as well as continual refining and improvement of present services.

Above: *A Mirrlees Generator set.*
Left: *An aerial view of the firm's site on Old Bawtry Road, Finningley.*
Facing page, top right: *A Ruston Generator set.*

Doncaster's 'one-stop' supplier to the catering trade

Formed in 1890, Braim & Cooper has remained an independent family business. The company's original trade was bone crushing, from which glue and bone meal were manufactured. In 1914 its 'founding fathers' began to concentrate on the production of edible oils and fats for the fish and chip trade. Today these are the firm's main products.

Some 45 years ago Braim was acquired by Mr Kenneth Mansfield who is still a company director. His son John is managing director and Mr John Mansfield's son, Duncan is now a director. The firm served the needs of the original fast food take-always but presently it supplies literally anyone connected with the catering trade.

To satisfy this demanding market the company has come up with an ever-increasing range of products. Claiming to be a 'one-stop supplier', the firm's stock includes oils and fats, flours and butter mixes, canned goods, soft drinks, condiments, sauces and pickles and a range of frozen foods. They also supply catering equipment from a chip scoop to a complete kitchen.

The staff are dedicated professionals with a tradition of long and loyal service. Customers too are loyal, many of them second or third generation family owned caterers who appreciate Braim & Cooper's traditional values and personal service.

The company's buildings are surrounded by peaceful fields. Inside, though, they are purely 1990s with frequently updated, computerised equipment and machinery. A fleet of modern, multi-functional vehicles ensure rapid delivery of goods to the company's many customers.

In 1994 the company was awarded the ISO 9002. Its creed, 'Quality, reliability and service', has kept it on course for more than a century and will be the key to sustained growth throughout the nineties and beyond.

Above: *The sales force outside headquarters.*
Left: *The peaceful rural setting of the company buildings circa 1950.*

Stringers' Nurseries - a growing business

Before he joined the armed forces, Mr Bob Stringer was in service as a gardener. In 1947, after the war, he decided to use that early experience by branching out on his own and setting up a market garden at what was the family home in Conisborough.

He produced field-grown crops of vegetables and cut flowers, mostly manually planted. In these early days, trees and shrubs could only be sold with bare roots. Today they are containerised and can be sold all the year round. Bob's wife, Eirene, joined him in the business after their marriage in 1950.

Alongside the garden work, Bob had market stalls in Doncaster and Denaby which were run by his brother Sam and Sam's wife Ethel. The firm also owned a greengrocery business and a florist's shop in Conisborough village until 1977.

Later, Bob and Eirene's daughter, Carol and her husband Michael took over the day to day running of things, becoming partners in 1987. Daughter Susan is an on-site florist and grand-daughter Annette is training as office accounts manager.

Past crop experiments, to name a few, have included mushrooms, lettuce, chrysanthemums and radishes.

It is still all hard work and an ever-growing team of loyal staff helps with the work load. Today most processes have been mechanised. There is a potting machine and mechanised planting equipment to increase plant production.

The business has always tried to be self-sufficient, doing as much of the building and construction work as possible. This was especially useful in 1984 when, on Friday, January 13th, a hurricane struck destroying a large section of the nursery. The original site has been considerably extended over the years with the building of a new Garden Centre Shop in 1994.

School visits are welcomed in spring and children as young as four have been shown the different jobs in progress and learned how things grow. Adults who would like to know more about what goes on would do well to read Mr Bob Stringer's book, 'Three Score and Ten', which gives a detailed history of the origin of the garden centre. It is on sale in the shop.

The business is scrupulous about accurate labelling and quality. It offers variety, honest advice and friendly service and would rather lose a sale than a customer.

***Above:** The market lorry pictured in 1991.*
***Left:** Stringer's Garden Centre, Doncaster.*
***Top:** A child plays outside the premises in the early days*
***Above left:** An aerial view that shows all operations before redevelopments.*

Walkers Solicitors - a comforting presence in Doncaster since the 1760s

The first person in their history of whom Walkers have any trace was Joseph Marris. Law Society Records do not go back that far, but he must have been a lawyer since deeds he prepared are still extant. Nothing else is known about him except that he was Clerk to Everton Internal Drainage Board. Walkers still act as solicitors and clerks to the Board - maybe the longest solicitor-client relationship ever.

The early days

Marris's legal practice was established in about 1760. He would have been called an attorney then. He worked from premises in the Bawtry High Street, though not the firm's present offices. John Cartwright became his partner in 1795 and his family kept the practice for the next hundred years. Another lawyer, Francis Raynes lived at the first house in Bawtry, 'Number One, Yorkshire'. His legal career spanned the period 1830-90. He was regarded as a bit of an upstart by the Cartwrights who must have been prominent citizens since their memorials can be seen in Bawtry Parish Church. The second Cartwright died in harness in 1881, leaving six daughters but no sons and his widow quickly sold up.

"WALKERS HAD THE SECOND TELEPHONE LINE IN BAWTRY - THE NUMBER BEING BAWTRY 2."

The Walker family connection

The buyer was John Walker. Born at Mattersey Hall in 1853, he qualified as a solicitor in about 1876. He had worked as an assistant in Rugby and Whitehaven but wanted a partnership in his home area. When he bought the Bawtry practice he was an assistant with Mr Burton of Gainsborough, but left when he found that the partnership had been promised elsewhere.

Joseph Marris
First recorded as Clerk (1764)

John Cartwright
(Joined Joseph Marris)

Frederick Hawksley Cartwright (died 1881)
joined his father

John Walker (died 1949)
Joined FH Cartwright - name changed to Cartwright & Walker

John Wickham Walker (killed in action 1916)
joined his father, John Walker - name changed to Walker & Son

Evelyn Degory Walker
Joined his father, John Walker

JA Walker
Joined his father, Evelyn Walker - retired but still an active consultant with the firm. His son Daniel is also a solicitor (the fourth generation) although not with this firm

Edward Burroughs
Joined John Walker as assistant in 1969 - now senior partner

Andrew Williamson
Joined the firm as articled clerk in 1978 - now a partner

Large areas of the countryside, and a lot of town properties as well, were then in the hands of the landed gentry. Most private houses, farms and business premises were rented. A country legal practice was very different from today. There was comparatively little conveyancing, and most of the courts were in larger towns. The better-off had wills made and looked to their lawyer for business and financial advice. Some very respectable money lending went on. Apart from the Drainage Board, a principal source of income was acting as steward of various manors, Gringley for the Duke of Portland, Tickhill for the Earl of Scarborough and Austerfield for the Earl of Crew. There was also the rent-collecting and other steady sources of income.

Those were leisured times. John Walker thought nothing of taking a whole day to visit a client in

Above: *The chronology of the firm, starting from the 1760s.*
Top left: *The first John Walker, who died in 1949.*

the country in his horse and trap. He had assistants, and simply had no need to work as hard as a modern solicitor. Walkers had the second telephone line in Bawtry, the original number being Bawtry 2.

The First World War
For continuity the firm was called Cartwright & Walker until 1912. John Walker's eldest son, John Wickham Walker, then joined it and it became Walker & Son. He had left school at 17 and had done the usual five years training as an articled clerk. He was only with the firm for two years before going off to fight and was killed in 1916, following his younger brother Anthony, who had been killed the year before.

By 1918 John Walker was 65 and his third son, Evelyn, was 19. He served his time as an articled clerk partly with his father and partly in London. He was made a partner as soon as he qualified in 1925. There was at least one assistant solicitor as well, though retrenchment came with the thirties recession.

Expansion in the depression
However, even in the thirties the firm prospered reasonably well. Since Tickhill Urban District Council was created in 1894, first John and later Evelyn Walker had been its Clerk. They thereby acquired a number of Tickhill clients for whom the firm still acts. Walker & Son was now the only firm of solicitors in Bawtry, with branches in Tickhill and Doncaster. Wilfred Duckworth joined the firm as clerk in the 1930s. He remained as managing clerk until his retirement in 1981.

The crunch came in World War II when all legal work was greatly reduced, especially as Evelyn Walker did virtually no litigation of any sort, regarding it as rather beneath him. Mr Duckworth was away in the Army (eventually becoming a Major) and the office just ticked over. After the war the firm profited from the establishment of the RAF Command HQ at Bawtry Hall and from the general move towards home ownership. John Walker died in harness in 1949, aged 95, the oldest practicing solicitor in the country. The same year David Stevenson joined the firm as junior clerk and is still there as a legal executive 49 years later.

Evelyn's son, another John Walker joined the firm as articled clerk in 1960. Soon afterwards, Evelyn fell ill leaving John to carry the main burden. 'The best training I could have had,' he asserts. He became a partner in 1963, immediately after qualifying.

The Tickhill Office
John Walker senior established an office in Tickhill before 1890. It continued as a branch office until 1965, manned for most of that period by Mr Maurice Hulley. Mr Hulley worked at 23 Westgate from 1919 until his retirement in 1960, doing a lot of conveyancing. Later it became more convenient to do the Tickhill work from Bawtry and Mr Hulley concentrated on Tickhill UDC work.

Tickhill UDC
Tickhill was the smallest place in England to have an Urban District Council. All its officials and employees were part time except the refuse men. The Council was run on a shoestring but was extremely efficient. Under Evelyn Walker as Clerk, it was one of the first authorities to have a purpose-built caravan site, and had one of the

Above: *The firm's premises in Bawtry, the home of Walkers Solicitors for over 150 years.*

shortest housing waiting lists in the country. When Evelyn Walker retired, John offered to succeed him but the Council decided to appoint a full time Clerk instead. The firm continued to act as solicitors for the Council until it was absorbed into the Doncaster MBC in 1974.

The modern Firm

Under John Walker the firm grew to an extent that he could no longer manage alone. In 1969 Edward Burroughs joined him as an assistant to build up the litigation and family work that had been almost ignored up to then. Edward Burroughs was the son of a Retford solicitor, and eventually the two firms were to merge. He became a partner in 1972, and is now the senior partner, concentrating on conveyancing, probate and tax. Andrew Williamson came to the firm in 1978 as an articled clerk and has remained ever since. He specialises in accident and medical claims, and has also masterminded the firm's transition to modern technology and management methods. It was thanks to him that the firm was the first in the region to gain certification to the management standard ISO 9001.

Above: *Evelyn Walker.*
Left: *Present Partners, Edward Burroughs (larger picture) and Andrew Williamson.*
Below: *Evelyn's son, John at his retirement party in the early 1990s, pictured her with his wife Sarah and some of the staff.*